P9-CDE-855

PRAISE FOR *The Point of Vanishing*

"Axelrod lyrically captures the essence of nature as he ponders his own self-worth and purpose in life. . . . In his first book, the author pushes beyond the boundaries and safety nets of the modern world and opens a doorway to feelings and experiences many long for but never encounter. His writing is a balm for world-weary souls. A vibrant, honest, and poetic account of how two years of solitude surrounded by nature changed a man forever."

Kirkus Reviews, starred review

"A sensitive and sensual book about seeing and feeling deeply; witty, wise, and beautifully written from beginning to end. When a debilitating accident rocks his world, Axelrod finds himself in free fall, the gleaming trajectory of his successful life suddenly tarnished and unclear. In documenting his retreat to a snowy solitude and the lessons learned there, Axelrod creates a surprisingly suspenseful narrative. I was constantly torn between wanting to savor his prose and tear through the pages to learn what happened next."

GERALDINE BROOKS, author of *March*

"Out of sudden and profound loss, Axelrod has drawn a haunting, tender memoir that grips like an emotional thriller. *The Point of Vanishing* is raw, exquisitely written, and full of poetic insights. This is a big book about big truths that matter to us all. It delivers a message of hope and strength, and reveals what is most human in our most unspoken yearning for something real, something true."

BELLA POLLEN, author of *The Summer of the Bear*

"Deeply alive and exciting and nuanced, a story of injury and years alone in the woods, *The Point of Vanishing* is all about what it means to see, and how we might ask ourselves to see differently—to live differently in our own bodies, and in the world. Though this book is set largely in the snow and silence, there are embers of hunger and questioning and longing that glow deep in its core and refuse to be cooled. Their heat charges and illuminates every moment of these pages. Powerful and ineffable, it feels like a blessing."

LESLIE JAMISON, author of *The Empathy Exams*

"This is a very real book, in bone-on-bone contact with the actual world. It made me think about my own life in new ways, and I think it will do the same for you."

BILL MCKIBBEN, author of *Deep Economy*

"Blindness and insight are the twin subjects of Howard Axelrod's intricate and beautiful memoir of his two years of solitude. In detailing his growing estrangement from 'ordinary' life, Axelrod offers a vision of what most of us take for granted. The unimportant falls away, in this book, and what comes closer is a luminous sense of the essential, the beautiful, the sacred, and the unspeakable."

CHARLES BAXTER, author of *The Feast of Love*

The Point of Vanishing

THE

Point

OF

Vanishing

a memoir of
two years in solitude

Howard Axelrod

Fitchburg Public Library
5530 Lacy Road
Fitchburg, WI 53711

Beacon Press, Boston

Beacon Press
Boston, Massachusetts
www.beacon.org

Beacon Press books
are published under the auspices of
the Unitarian Universalist Association of Congregations.

© 2015 by Howard Axelrod
All rights reserved
Printed in the United States of America

18 17 16 15   8 7 6 5 4 3

This book is printed on acid-free paper that meets the uncoated paper
ANSI/NISO specifications for permanence as revised in 1992.

Text design and composition by Wilsted & Taylor

Some names and identifying characteristics of people mentioned
in this work have been changed to protect their identities.

Tomas Tranströmer, excerpt from "Preludes," translated by Robert Bly,
from *The Half-Finished Heaven: The Best Poems of Tomas Tranströmer*.
Copyright © 2001 by Tomas Tranströmer. Translation copyright © 2001 by
Robert Bly. Reprinted with the permission of The Permissions Company, Inc.,
on behalf of Graywolf Press, Minneapolis, MN, http://www.graywolfpress.org.

Library of Congress Cataloging-in-Publication Data

Axelrod, Howard.
    The point of vanishing : a memoir of two years in solitude / Howard Axelrod.
    pages cm
    ISBN 978-0-8070-7546-3 (paperback : acid-free paper)
    ISBN 978-0-8070-7547-0 (ebook)
    1. Axelrod, Howard, 1973– 2. Young men—United States—Biography. 3. People
with visual disabilities—United States—Biography. 4. Eye—Wounds and injuries—Patients—United States—Biography. 5. Vision, Monocular—Psychological
aspects. 6. Axelrod, Howard, 1973—Homes and haunts—Vermont. 7. Solitude—
Psychological aspects. 8. Visual perception. 9. Self-perception. 10. Vermont—
Biography. I. Title.
    CT275.A95245A3 2015
    614.5'997092—dc23
    [B]   2015004216

For my parents

Two truths approach each other. One comes from inside,
the other from outside,
and where they meet, we have a chance to catch sight of
ourselves.

—Tomas Tranströmer, from "Preludes,"
translated by Robert Bly

Contents

Prologue

The house wasn't something you stumbled upon by accident. It wasn't something you passed going anywhere else. To get there you drove through Glover, Vermont—a general store, no traffic light, one Busy Bee Diner—climbed along switchbacks through maples, evergreens, and birches, then turned left onto a wide dirt road. You passed the barn and blue silo of the Mooreland dairy farm, snaked past a few scattered houses and trailers, then followed deeper into the woods, the maples tapped, tubed, and strung together like prisoners on a chain gang, as it was early March now, sugar season. A few miles in, at a mailbox nobody used, you forked off the wide dirt road onto an unmaintained narrow lane, the deeper snow tugging at your car as though part of a different gravity. You slipped through a tunnel of overhanging trees, came to an empty field bordered by tall pines, then passed an uninhabited house, its siding job left unfinished, then followed as the road dwindled into what seemed only the ghost of a road—no car tracks but your own, the twin trail in the snow behind you like a vestige of the two ruts in summer, when the weeds between them would grow taller than your hood. A small meadow opened on your left, three gnarled apple trees glimmering in the sunlight like chandeliers, and beyond the meadow was the beginning again of forest, with little promise of a house at all. From there, just inside the buried fenceposts, you walked. And at the bottom of the steep grade, with its sky-blue paint flaking, its lines badly canted, sat the two-story house, like a sunken ship.

I

Not much from the outside world found me there. In the year and a half since I'd moved in, there had never been a knock on the door. I had no television, no computer, no cell phone. There was a land line, which rang maybe twice a month, so a wrong number was an event. As for other news, the yellowing issues of the *Newport Chronicle*, stacked in the corner by the woodstove, reported on beaver problems, church suppers, DWI charges, and missing dogs, but all from years past. Sometimes, kindling the fire's embers at dawn, I'd find myself wondering about *a handsome spotted pointer* or *the cutest darn black mutt you ever saw*. But then I'd notice the newspaper's date: those dogs had lighted out for their canine dreams two summers earlier, long before the snows.

The only news that didn't reach me with a kind of ghostliness came through the house's windows or from my daily walks up into the woods. Clouds wrestling on a blustery afternoon, sunlight opening through the birches as though from behind a curtain. Slow flurries descending towards dusk. And about once a week, if the roads were clear, I'd make the drive down into the town of Barton for groceries at the C&C, then up the curving road to the Lake Parker General Store. West Glover's tiny post office hid at the back of the store, in an elevator-sized room with bars and a window, as though it had once been the town's tiny bank. The young woman behind the counter was no more than eighteen, lovely and bovine in her slowness. She would walk the dirt-worn floorboards very deliberately, past the cooler full of milk, past the six packs of beer, past the canned goods, then enter the post office and check the box for General Delivery. Not wanting to make her any more self-conscious, or myself any more aware of what it would mean to be alone with a woman again, I'd wait up at the counter. When she returned, she'd blush like something blooming in one of those time-lapse nature movies, the red rising up her neck, then her cheek, the blush all the more vivid when there was no mail for me. Maybe this was because I looked something like a wild animal—shaggy beard, eyes too intense. Or maybe it was just because my voice had gone unused since my last trip to the store, and, when I thanked her, too much feeling was stored up inside it. Even to me, my words seemed to come from far away, as though they required travel time, like light from a distant star.

So on that moonless March night, when three raps came at the mudroom door, surprise wasn't the word for my response. Each rap sounded alarmingly *inside* the house, hardening the posts and beams into place. A current ran through my body—a rattling, physical charge. The blue candle guttered on the table. It seemed I was underwater and something was bobbing on the surface far above me. In the darkened windows to the woods, the reflection of my dinner flickered soft and shadowy, more the idea of a dinner than anything solid. And my image flickered just the same.

On my weekly trip to the C&C, I was prepared, knowing I would be seen: reflections, however glancing, would be cast back at me from the check-out girl snapping her gum (*hippie*), from the bulky matrons trundling their carts (*drifter*)—reflections bearable because they seemed so obviously wrong. But the thought of someone there, as close as the mudroom door, was like a mirror flashed close to my face. A man alone, a barely furnished room, a candle on the table. The scene like an ancient interrogation but with no visible interrogator. The downstairs bathroom did have a mirror, but I never confronted it—not brushing my teeth, not washing my face, not stepping out of the shower. Not because I minded my face itself, or even my blind right eye, which had developed a pearly green cataract since my accident, but because the gaunt twenty-five-year-old man in the mirror was no one I recognized. A figure was there, a physical presence, but he followed me only at a distance. Even keeping a journal had come to feel strange—as though I was trying to sketch my own outline, to corral the wind, the snow, and the stars into the shape of a man. Coming to the woods hadn't been an exercise or a retreat—it wasn't something to take notes on and jar for later, like summer berries. I needed to live without the need of putting on a face for anyone, including myself. I needed to be no one, really, while carrying the hope that my particular no one might feel familiar, might turn out to be someone I had known all along—the core of who I'd been as boy, the core of who I might become as a man. Beneath all the masks I'd accumulated over the years, beneath even the masks that resented those masks, there had to be something there, something essential, some sense of reality and of myself that couldn't be broken.

The knocking came again, the same three sharp raps. Standing frozen by the woodstove, I pictured the night outside. The last stretch of road to the house so narrow, the snow six feet deep, the passage like a bobsled run. The darkness mitigated only by the stars. The only people I'd seen in the nearby hills, apart from Nat and his son, who occasionally came to plow the unmaintained lane, were deer hunters. But hunting season was months gone. The winter sun had long since set. Whoever was at the door had to be more frightened than I was. If there was a crazy man in the woods, a wild bearded loner liable to do anything, I was him. *I am the crazy man! I am the crazy man!* It was the same thing I'd told myself so many times hearing a branch snap in the woods or the stairs creak in the middle of the night. *I am the crazy man! I am the crazy man!* Usually, it hardened my fear into something like resolve. But now I couldn't help picturing a middle-aged man in a checked wool jacket, slouching at the door. A glowing cigarette in one hand, a rifle in the other. And no deer for miles.

The three raps came again, more insistent. It was probably an emergency, someone was probably in need. Smoke was rising from my chimney. Candlelight spilled out onto the snow. There really wasn't much of a choice. I stepped into my moccasins, crossed the plywood mudroom floor, and opened the door.

PART I

Into the Blind Spot

I

It felt like a homecoming. It didn't matter that a thunderstorm was raging, the rain drumming on the tar-paper roof, gunpowder flashes lighting up the dense, dripping foliage behind the house. It didn't matter that I hadn't stocked up yet at the C&C, so my dinner was only a piece of toast with melted cheese. And it didn't matter that Boston was hundreds of miles away—and had stopped feeling like my home years earlier. My one frying pan sat on the stove. My two forks, two knives, and two spoons were installed in the drawer by the sink. My sweaters, wool socks, and snowpants were unpacked on the plywood shelves upstairs. And outside, at the top of the steep dirt grade, my little white Honda sat empty. I pictured it like a pack horse finally unburdened, its body wild and calm with relief. It had known some beautiful pastures since my college graduation three years earlier—elk plodding through a drifting snow in the Grand Tetons; the mesa late in the day gone ochre and purple above the Rio Grande—but for the first time, it would be in one place longer than four months. There would be no need to leave, no need to pack my bags again, no need to search elsewhere. Lev, the owner of the house, wouldn't be back until June. Finally, I could allow myself not to be an outsider, to belong to the land.

I'd found the house by posting handwritten signs across northern Vermont, on the quilt-like bulletin boards outside general stores, on the musty walls inside laundromats, in Peacham, Johnson, Jay, in Barton, Newport, and Morrisville, and even in one town called Eden. My attempt at respectable handwriting hung there beside the firewood for sale, the beloved lost cats, the spaghetti dinners already weeks gone: *Wanted: a cabin or house set in the woods, with good light, very solitary. Proximity to a stream or brook. Running water and electricity preferred.* Only one man had replied. Lev was a philosophy professor, leaving in September to teach in his native Tel Aviv. He'd bought the house the previous summer and was refurbishing it. In August, I made the six-hour drive from Boston, and Lev took me on a tour, pointing out his meager renovations. He was surprisingly tall, with a reddish beard and restless hands. It was hard to see the house through his talking. He'd planned to take sabbaticals with his wife, but after one winter of solitude for two, they were divorcing. He'd never lived in the house alone. He said he greatly anticipated such a winter—*God only comes to those who are alone*, he said—but it was obvious from his combination of bluster and warning that he viewed me as a guinea pig. I didn't mind; the guinea pig rate was good. I'd only have to pay for six cords of firewood, electricity, and a bit of propane for the hot-water heater—less than one thousand dollars all told.

From the outside, the house resembled a battered pirate ship run aground. A glass look-out tower, small slanting decks with sagging wooden railings, a catwalk along the second story, its two planks noticeably bowed. Doubling as the hold was a makeshift garage—a corrugated steel roof sloped over a dirt floor, the berths not large enough for cars but well-suited for storing firewood. Inside, through the mudroom, the main room was no less jerry-rigged—the lightbulb above the table exposed, half the floor plywood, half faux-wood flooring—but it wasn't a cave, wasn't damp or dark. There were three floor-to-ceiling windows offering a kind of triptych of the woods. There was a refrigerator, an electric stove, a toaster oven. There was a woodstove for heat. Up a steep set of wooden stairs was the bedroom—with wide wood floorboards, a sloping ceiling, and a mattress in the corner. On the far side of the mattress was Lev's pride and joy: a small raised office space, with a desk and commanding view of the Green Mountains. The window looked out above one of the pitched and beaten decks. The green hills retreated into the distance like cresting waves.

"Nine months," Lev had said, as we looked out. "You move in October 1. You go into the Vermont winter and through it. You are certain you can manage?"

I nodded.

"In these woods time plays tricks on you."

"I understand."

He wanted me to understand, but he didn't want me to understand, he wanted to explain. "Your timing sense changes."

"Sure," I said. I was picturing an air filter from a car, the closest my mind could come to a timing belt, which was the closest I could come to picturing *timing sense*. Since my eye accident, I tended to see what I heard, even if the picture only confused me.

"Make sure to study the manual I leave you. Remember what I tell you about the creosote in the chimney. And shoveling the roof. And the toilets freezing. Freezing, it is possible."

Lastly, as we went back downstairs, he admitted that the house was a strange one. It was built in the '70s by a hippie from New York, a man who suffered from an almost pathological fear of war. The man had constructed a bomb shelter in the basement, a cinderblock crypt reached by a staircase that was hidden below a panel in the floor.

Finally ready to humor Lev, now that he was across the Atlantic and the house was mine, I pushed aside my toast and opened the manual he'd written. As I read, lightning flared outside, the yellow birch leaves exploding like thousands of dressing room lightbulbs. The pines flashed deep blue. A roll of thunder rumbled under the floorboards. The rain went on describing the house, introducing the roof and the windows. It was soothing to hear my shelter, to feel its shape around me. That seemed like the real manual, the one I'd have to learn day by day in the months ahead.

The typed manual was eighteen pages long. There were lists, there were histories, there were warnings. There was the painfully obvious: *Do not use the toilet if toilet water has frozen.* There was the painfully insignificant: *The woodstove is the Jotul brand, from Sweden, and is very respected.* There was the painfully loud: DO NOT ALLOW WOODSTOVE TO GO ABOVE 700 DEGREES, CHIMNEY COULD CATCH FIRE AND EXPLODE. CHECK RED DEVIL GAUGE ON LEFT SIDE OF STOVE FREQUENTLY!

The hazards kept coming. I could slip off the roof. I could get snowed in for weeks without food. I could encounter a bear *right outside the house.* I felt as though I was stumbling over the frozen corpses of men strewn along the path up Everest, this one ravaged by obsessiveness, that one undone by loneliness, this one overtaken by fear. It wasn't a manual on how to care for the house so much as an inadvertent primer on the dangers of solitude. For company you could surround yourself with potential threats, so you didn't have to recognize the larger threat of simply being alone. THE THREAT OF SILENCE. THE THREAT OF NO DISTRACTIONS.

The manual annoyed me. I didn't want Lev as a model. I didn't want any anxious chatter inside my head. And, besides, I'd come here for that silence: a silence that might enable me to hear more, which might enable me to see more. I needed that expansiveness in the house, and I needed it in the woods around the house—even if it meant a great loneliness would come, too.

As I kept flipping the pages, growing afraid to miss something actually important, a kind of fissure opened inside me, a weakness unstringing through my ribs. I knew what it meant to be too alone, knew how that bone-deep loneliness could begin to fuzz your mind. I knew how you could lose your sense of direction, not just of north, south, east, and west but of something more basic, something having to do with your own sturdiness in the world. Your own sense of what was solid.

Time in the woods plays tricks on you. The lightning went again, the millions of tiny lightbulbs in the leaves less spectacular, the thunder slow to follow. The green candles flickered on the table, their shadows anchoring them to the tablecloth. The thinness was still whistling through my ribs.

I stood up from the table, stowed the booklet in a low cupboard beneath the sink. I didn't want to feel it close by, all those caps and bold letters, all that arm waving. I didn't want to be reminded of all the ways solitude could go wrong. And I didn't want to think about what would happen if I couldn't find solid ground here, if I couldn't find anything I could trust—or how I'd already driven across the country twice looking for answers, or how I was running out of money, out of options, out of land. After a moment, I took the booklet out from the cupboard, ripped off the back page with the important phone numbers, and fed the rest into the fire in the woodstove. The torn pages caught and crumpled in the flames. I needed this too much. Lev's fear, I promised myself, would not be mine.

Your life changes in an instant. When it does, it splits into two different lives, with two different timelines, the bridge between Before and After exploded in the very moment of its making, the force of that explosion throwing you indefinitely to the other side. There are questions on that other side—questions about the very nature of what is real, what is important, and what is worth living for. You have to answer them. You have no choice. You can't go back to Before. To open the ripped sky into some deeper sky behind it, you have to answer.

It was a fine blue-sky afternoon, early May. As I trotted down the stairs of Adams House, the musty stairwell aired by intermittent sunlight, there was nowhere I had to be, nothing in particular I had to do. I was twenty years old. Finals for my junior year at Harvard were three weeks away. Summer winked from the distance: mornings without classes, books read for pleasure, an editorship waiting for me at *Let's Go*, the student-written travel guide. Not that I particularly wanted to be a travel guide editor, but it seemed something to try for, an almost-real job.

The gym was mostly empty—the resounding echo of a few balls, a few guys shooting on the three courts. The gym always made me feel at home, if a little guilty for having so much time on my hands. My friends Ray and Alexis spent their afternoons down at the chem lab, already on the long trail towards becoming doctors; my roommate, Andrew, was either on the tennis courts, training for a professional career, or in Lamont Library drilling himself for his classes, compensating for the time he lost to the courts. But my afternoons were still a kind of waiting room: writing an occasional music review for *The Crimson*, doing a little volunteer work, going to the gym. That was the privilege of being an English major. Besides, it was only the end of junior year, my grades were nearly all A's, and I was in no hurry. The given career options as presented over the years by my family had always been lawyer, doctor, or businessman—like a child's game with firemen and policemen but the suburban version. Dad, my uncle, my aunt, and my cousin were all lawyers, and my older brother, Matt, was on his way.

I'd spent so many hours playing basketball in high school, and devoted so many hours to watching the Celtics with Matt at home on the couch, that playing pick-up games was more than just a way of relaxing from the career track I hadn't found. To rise into a baseline jumper, to slash through the lane, was like flipping through a scrapbook of my past—my muscles still carrying those late afternoons in the high school gym, the snowstorms Matt and I had played through in the backyard, fingers going numb. The way holidays carry vestiges of holidays past, that's what basketball was for me. Every time I picked up a ball, the leather on my fingertips reintroduced me to all those hours with other basketballs, on other courts, with other people, which was always a quiet reminder of who I was.

We shot for teams, ran one quick game to 11, but everyone else needed to get back to studying. As guys began filtering out of the gym, a stocky red-haired guy called over to me. He cradled a basketball on his hip like a clipboard. "We need one more," he said. "It'll just take fifteen minutes. You want in?"

As I hesitated at the doorway, keys already in my hand, all I felt was a kind of aimlessness. It didn't really matter if I stayed for one more game or if I left. The only thing waiting for me back in my room in Adams was daydreaming—and weren't you supposed to stop daydreaming as you got older? Or maybe daydreaming wasn't even the word. It had just happened again on my bed after lunch. I was reading a poem for class, written by a twelfth-century Japanese woman named Izumi Shikibu.

> If he whom I wait for
> Should come now, what will I do?
> This morning the snow-covered garden
> Is so beautiful without a trace of footprints.

I glanced up, looked around my room, as if to make sure no one had seen—which was ridiculous, since my face probably betrayed nothing, not to mention I was alone. But it was for this very reason that I never studied in the library. Around me, I could feel the far hills softened by snow, the feathery quiet of the morning. I could feel that sudden hollow inside the woman's chest—the way she wanted her lover to come, of course she wanted him to come, but the way the new snow was pristine, the way it touched the part of herself she trusted most. We were supposed to consider the difference between this poem and a haiku, to contrast the forms. And I'd get to that in a moment, do it routinely, but for now I just wanted to sit with her—with the wind at her hair, with the cool, shivery smoothness of her skin beneath her kimono, with the feeling of sex not far off, and the way she probably knew her fear was both very childish and very mature at the same time. Then I heard footsteps pounding up the stairs of the entryway, a door slamming, and I was shamed back to my assignment, back to my pen bleeding onto the comforter.

"So what are the teams?" I said, stepping back onto the court.

Peter, who looked like Abraham Lincoln minus the beard, paired up with me—tall, gangly, all elbows and knees. We'd played together before and I liked our chances. He needed to be in motion not to look awkward, but he had an automatic jump shot, was fast, and he knew the game. The redhead's teammate had a massive upper body and stick legs, like the front cab of an eighteen wheeler with no rig.

The other courts were empty and the game began—quiet, workmanlike, the satisfying echo of the dribble, the tick of the leather in and out of hands. Peter and I were ahead, the redhead and his teammate no match for Peter's deft back-door passing. But about midway through the game, Peter took a jump shot from the right wing. The shot hit the front of the rim and angled sharply back towards the foul line. We all darted for the ball. I was ahead of the redhead, but Peter and the little truck were also converging. For a moment, the ball hovered there, suspended. I remember the feeling of being too close, of space seeming to collapse among the bodies. And then the pain.

The gym fell quiet. I stayed down on the court, not moving. The sensation was unlike anything—so deep, so internal, that I didn't know what to do. If I'd twisted my ankle, been kneed in the balls, I would have known the protocol: assess the damage, then limp off the court or keep playing. But a liquid, it was blood, was beginning to drip onto my face, onto my t-shirt. And the pain was something I couldn't locate. It was too interior, like something had gone wrong inside my skull. Like some kind of acid had dripped behind my eye.

Very slowly, Peter helped me off the court, led me down the stairs.

Outside the gym, the daylight was shattering. My eye had already swollen shut, and to my left eye the world appeared a provisional version of itself—the brick sidewalk, Lowell House across the street—none of it firmly in place, the sunlight filtering through the trees as though from no one source, everything overly bright. The wide stone steps of the gym shimmered like water, each step solid only as it formed under my foot, one step, then the next. Space in general felt wider, less confined, but the space around me felt tighter. As though I was on a lower frequency than everyone else, existing in some range that human ears couldn't hear.

Peter followed beside me towards University Health Services, but I avoided looking at him. It had been his finger that had hooked into my eye. My hand trailed instinctively along the brick wall that lined the narrow sidewalk. The day was too bright. There was nowhere to look. A constant bee sting burned at the back of my eyeball, surrounded by a tight-fist throbbing. My t-shirt was stained with streaks of blood, and anger was pushing through my veins. A tight feeling of wanting to strike back, to throw parked cars out of my way. *Why had this happened? Why had this happened to me?* I told myself it was just music playing in a neighboring room, just something to ignore. But I could feel so much swimming, so many emotions swirling and darting, some barrier between me and the deepest waters suddenly disappeared. Vaguely, I admitted to myself time might be a factor but didn't admit to myself for what. Below that, as Peter and I crossed Mount Auburn Street—its two lanes suddenly horrible and dazzling—I tried to ignore the angry appeal already buzzing inside me: *I can do better, give me another chance.*

At University Health Services, a doctor swabbed some of the blood away from my eye and pressed with his thumb around the lid. He was probably in his sixties. He introduced himself as Dr. Hardenbergh. He'd seen all this before, it seemed. Maybe my senses were heightened, but his white coat smelled like mothballs. His office was straight out of Norman Rockwell. He said he was going to snip something, it wouldn't hurt, and just over the bridge of my nose, with my left eye, I saw him cut something white, like a bit of boiled egg. It didn't hurt—he was right. Maybe it was just the eye's version of dead skin. But that something could be cut from my eye, and with so little explanation, was not reassuring.

After a quick examination of each eye with his penlight, Dr. Hardenbergh switched the overhead light back on. "Very good," he said.

I didn't move.

"You can go back to your dorm room. You'll have quite a shiner." He peeled off his rubber gloves.

"I can't see anything in my right eye."

"Just heavy swelling. Nothing to worry about. In less than a week the eye should open."

I had the strange sensation of desperately wanting to believe something I knew wasn't true. "When you put your penlight in my eye, I didn't see anything."

Dr. Hardenbergh removed his penlight again. His bare fingers forced my bruised lid open. "You really don't see anything?"

"No. I really don't."

"Surprising. You'll want to go down to the Mass Eye and Ear Infirmary. You know where it is? You can take the subway. The Red Line."

"Are you kidding me?"

Dr. Hardenbergh went to the sink, began to wash his hands. "Why would I be kidding?"

"Time isn't a factor? Can you tell me time isn't a factor?"

"No ambulance necessary. If that's what you mean."

Physical anger blared through my body. I wanted to grab the doctor by his white coat and slam him up against the wall. And behind the anger there lurked a sickening fear: I hadn't really been doing anything with my life, and now some outside factor was going to make it impossible for me to redeem myself. *Of those to whom much has been given, much is expected.* Didn't this doctor know who he was talking to? Didn't he know how much I had to do?

"No ambulance necessary. Not necessary. Because?"

"I can't call for one. Simple protocol."

I didn't trust this man. "Then get me a cab."

Dr. Hardenbergh stared at me.

"Now," I said.

I liked going outside to sit in the quiet. It was like wading into an ocean, the way it surrounded and held my legs, the way it made me heavier and lighter at the same time. My first few days, I could spend only so much time inside the house without going back to it.

It must have been my third or fourth morning. The front door, which was strangely medieval, made of heavy black iron and glass, opened to an unkempt ramble of land that sloped up unevenly towards the trees. A few rotten logs, a kind of token gesture at stairs, were wedged in among the knee-high grass, the daisy fleabane, the black-eyed susans. The single enormous oak tree had already turned deep copper, a thin skirt of leaves fallen around its base. I climbed up past its bulging roots to the highest point before the birches began. Out above the house's tarpaper roof and the spire-like tops of the spruces, the hills dazzled in a sweep of fall color, like a town with all ages on parade: the youthful, shimmering yellow; the abiding, stately green; the full-throated oranges and reds, all of it fading to harlequin corduroy, then to the mountains going blue in the distance. None of it was new, exactly. I'd stopped to appreciate the view every morning. But for some reason, the silence surrounded me now. It was tremendous in its completeness. I'd felt it before—when I first pulled in by the meadow, when I came back from stocking up at the C&C—but maybe my senses hadn't quite been able to travel at car speed, and now, given the extra couple days of only walking, my senses were beginning to arrive. To slow down and move in. In the past, whenever I'd been alone, there'd always been the possibility of another person—a kind of door held open in the silence for another person to enter. But now four or five miles separated me from the Mooreland farm, six or seven miles from the nearest main road. No one would be coming within miles of the house—not that afternoon, not that night, not the next day. No human noise, apart from my own breathing, would enter into what I was hearing.

It was hard to admit to myself how desperate I was to be here. My only plan, which felt more like survival instinct, was to return to a place where my senses felt at home. As a boy, I'd gone to an overnight camp in New Hampshire, just across the Connecticut River from Vermont. We played sports during the day, sang songs by the campfire at night, hiked in the White Mountains once a week. It was a place I couldn't remember without feeling it in my body. Every walk up to the soccer field carried the scent of sun-warmed blueberries; on the softball diamond you could smell the rain before you heard it sweeping over the hilltop, a strengthening patter until it was hammering towards you on the leaves. I liked to get up early, before anyone else in my cabin, and sneak out the door to sit on the porch. During the day, I was just like the other boys—saving my best polo shirt for Square Dance, making bets to win an extra Snickers bar on Candy Night, equally engaged in debates about the hottest girl in Bunk 19 and whether "the Garden" meant Madison Square Garden, where the Knicks played, or Boston Garden, where the Celtics did. But what I remember most vividly is those mornings. Behind me, through the screen windows, I could hear the soft sounds of my friends sleeping. The lake would be still as glass, just skeins of mist drifting across it, the morning light flashing green and gold. It was my first idea of how a lake should smell in the morning, of how a morning should look and feel— and my first feeling of fitting in with something larger than my friends, of fitting in with the world around me. It was my first glimpse of myself, really—not of myself preening in the mirror or trying to be like my friends, but my first glimpse of myself when the thing I thought of as myself was entirely quiet. Eventually, I'd steal back inside the cabin, not wanting to be caught being different, but as my friends did wake up, I'd try to carry that feeling into breakfast with them, into our activities. Some days it worked, and my perspective seemed as wide as the lake and the mountains, and some days it didn't. But those few minutes on the porch almost always returned me to that feeling in myself, to that quiet of already belonging—returned me to a place to start from with other people.

But now the silence, as it began to fill in, wasn't entirely silent. High up in the oak tree a breeze stirred. Lower, behind me, the same breeze swept through the maples and birches and sounded like a stream. The land began to feel like a room—only a room without ceiling or walls. Bounding into the foreground, a squirrel came ripping through the fallen leaves, every leap crisp and loud, as though the thrashing sounds were the source of his power, propelling him into his next leap. He stopped a few yards from me, whipped his bushy tail in quick liquid movements. He whipped and whipped. Then he bounded off, one smooth low sine curve into the trees. As my ears followed, I realized I'd been hearing space as much as sound—the dimensionality of the oak tree's branches, of the forest edge behind me, of the dry leaves on the grass, all of it so much more subtle than I could see. The day was teeming with road signs, with ways to orient myself in space. The acres and acres of wilderness were an invitation. A way to learn what was solid—in the world and in myself.

But later that afternoon, the rain falling again, all that space closed in on me. I was upstairs, wrestling a futon mattress from the spare room into the bedroom. I didn't want to keep sleeping on the mattress where Lev slept, didn't like feeling his body's impression when I lay down, didn't want to absorb whatever dreams he hadn't quite finished. Sweat prickled under my armpits. The futon had rubbed a little red patch on my cheek. It would have been so easy to lift the futon over the floor with the help of another person, but there was no other person. No neighbor, no friend down the hall. No chance of the most basic help. So I kept dragging. At the doorway the futon caught, slamming me into the doorjamb. I hadn't seen the floor wasn't flat. A scrape above my elbow began to bleed.

"Shit."

My voice sounded strange, disembodied. But something in my blood was racing. Since the accident, just being jostled on the sidewalk would throw my body into instant turmoil. About a month earlier in Boston, the strap of a man's backpack had slapped me on the cheek as he hurried off the subway. I'd felt an immediate urge to chase him down the platform, to tackle him on the full run. What I planned to say to him at that point, our limbs entangled, I had no idea. That part of the scene, when I reimagined it later, made me feel horrible, like I was a rabid dog desperate to spread my disease. Recognizing my body for the alarmist it had become, I always had to say to it: *You're really worried about a little slap, a stubbed toe, a jammed finger? You really think you can't heal? You really think this is permanent?* But that didn't mean the anger stopped coming. A body is stubborn that way.

I felt the primal surge now, a readiness to fight, and, below it, a shadow feeling of having been violated. *Stupid Lev, lonely troll, why didn't you fucking warn me about the ramshackle carpentry?* But, hearing my thoughts ricochet in the empty house, I knew I was being absurd. Completely my idea to move the mattress, completely my execution. I stood by the window foolishly. The rain kept whispering into the dark trees. There was no one for miles to blame. Maybe it was the first lesson of solitude: *everything really is your fault.*

In the bedroom, I dropped the futon with a loud slap on the floor. The blood continued to fork down my forearm, two jagged trails. *Two roads diverged in a yellow wood.* I finally managed a grim smile. This was just part of settling in, just start-up costs, and from now on, I reassured myself, things would go more smoothly.

But later in the night, the rain drumming on the roof and the pitched deck above the mattress, the noise of my own mind surrounded me. I started thinking about how the house made no sense. Three roofs, two of them flat, bound to be buried in snow. A front door, at the bottom of a steep pitch, bound to be buried, too. The triptych windows to the woods—beautiful but ideal for losing heat. The house clearly hadn't been designed by a Vermonter. Or even by a person capable of envisioning snow. I tried not to think about how my plan, if it even was a plan, was just as haphazardly formed. I tried not to think about Ray and

Alexis in med school in New York City, not to think about my parents, not to think about other places I might have been. And then there were the undercurrents, the background thoughts, the ones that had become a part of my mind's weather—the ones I didn't need to think about to feel. If only the basketball had come off the rim differently, if only I'd left the gym after the first game. And, of course, Milena. There was always Milena. Just the cool echo of her name, from those dark woods of not-thinking, carried the scent of my room in Bologna, of the thin blue blanket on the mattress, carried the sound of her voice, so foreign and so familiar in my ear. I couldn't allow myself to think about her. Couldn't allow the thought that she had punched my ticket to the woods as much as the accident had. That year in Italy after college had made it so hard to return to Boston, so easy to get in the car and head west, so easy to begin the descent into solitude. It was the two together, a delayed chemical reaction, an exponential loss.

But pushed from the room, my non-thoughts just slipped into the rain, and they gusted against the walls with tremendous force. The beams creaked. The floor seemed to pitch and yaw. The rain lashed at the window above my head. I imagined the morning sun finding me far out in the Atlantic, quietly bobbing, clutching a floorboard to my chest.

I lay awake, trying not to listen, the pillow over my ear. So much for opening my senses, for expanding and slowing down. So much for using my extra sensitivity as a new compass, as a way to get down to something real.

I wondered if I'd made a horrible mistake.

The only timeline I can be certain of is this: Peter's finger went into my eye around four in the afternoon; I left the hospital around two in the morning. Maybe with my sense of space gone uncertain, time had gone uncertain, too. Sometimes I rotated examining rooms, sometimes the doctors rotated to see me. Sometimes the wait was minutes, sometimes it seemed hours. Sometimes the waiting was a relief, sometimes it felt unendurable.

The only doctor I remember clearly was a young Pakistani man, probably just a resident. The small examining room was rinsed with air-conditioning. The doctor introduced himself in a soft voice and extracted magnifying lenses from a case lined with red velvet. His fingers were gentle on my cheekbone. He took his time peering into my eye. Given the amount of blood, he explained, getting a clear view was difficult. Then he pivoted the large examining apparatus, which looked like a periscope, so it was in front of me. "Chin on the bar, forehead against the curved plastic band."

I pushed forward.

"Come forward, please."

I pushed forward again. My eye was a peep show for his bright lights: pale blue concentric circles of light—that was to check my eye pressure. The terribly bright white light, like the headlamp of an oncoming train—that was to see in more detail. The doctor held my swollen eyelids open. It was impossible not to back away blinking. But the doctor waited. His manner calmed me some—an answer, it seemed, would be found. Then he brought out his penlight. He turned off the room light and had me cover my left eye with the palm of my hand. Again, he held open the swollen lids of my right eye.

"I want you to tell me if you see anything," he said into the darkness. "If you can tell when the light is on. Do you see anything?"

I could hear his breathing and the very faint rustle of his white coat. I could hear the clicking of his penlight, strangely loud, as though a whole auditorium's lights were being thrown on and off.

"Anything? Tell me when the light is on."

His accent was faintly British, his breath mildly freshened by gum. I could picture him standing there, could picture the look in his gentle brown eyes, as he watched my eye, as he waited for an answer. But in front of my open eye, there was just darkness—a dark tunnel, night in the darkest forest. I tried to focus closer, then farther away, but there was no closer, no farther away. It was the same kind of darkness I'd tried to imagine as a child before falling asleep—a kind of deep space, which for some reason I'd assumed would be relaxing, but then the darkness would usually turn into a blackboard, and random words would start appearing in chalk.

"Anything?"

The doctor was waggling the penlight back and forth—I was almost sure, from the rustling of his sleeve.

"Anything?" His voice bounced off the chair, off the floor, off the walls. I had the sensation of being a witness, but a witness who had lost the authority to speak. I heard his penlight, his sleeve, I *saw* them. But it was as though, without the right type of evidence, my testimony no longer mattered. I'd fallen somewhere below the visual, somewhere that couldn't be trusted.

"Nothing?" he said.

His sleeve had stopped moving. The penlight had clicked off.

"Nothing," I said.

After a moment, the doctor flipped the overhead light back on; he wheeled his stool over to my left-hand side. He explained that the retina of my right eye was detached and that my cornea was badly scratched. Normally, these were problems that could be fixed. But the real problem, he was sorry to say, was that the optic nerve behind my eye had been severed. Peter's finger had gone in past the knuckle and curved behind my eyeball, his fingernail slicing the nerve. The doctor showed me this on his own finger, pointing to his gold wedding band, which was a bit more information than I needed. Without an intact optic nerve, he explained, no information could be carried from my eye to my brain. Medical science did not yet know how to regenerate the optic nerve. Given the severity of the injury, he said, there was nothing that could be done.

"Do you have any questions?"

I did, but it seemed they weren't in my head, just as what I'd seen of his penlight hadn't been in my eyes.

"Anything?" he said.

"I don't think so."

"You're sure now?"

I felt a kind of vertigo. "No questions."

"We'll need to run a few tests. Do a CT scan to make sure there's no blood in your brain. But there shouldn't be anything else to worry about."

Nothing else to worry about.

I thanked him for his explanation, grateful for etiquette for the first time in my life—for its small dignity when there was nothing else to say.

2

Something was pressing into the bright stillness, a kind of approaching blur. Instinctively, I slipped through the tall grass to stand behind one of the apple trees. It was a mild day, the blond October sun touching off the loamy scent of the leaves, and I was barefoot—the grass cool and sharp in the shade. The truck noise interrupted the meadow first, its own cavalry of warning, and then the truck itself rounded the bend, a flatbed with wood slats on the sides. It jounced along the ruts, dirt rising in a slow cloud behind it. Watching from behind the tree, I felt my heart pounding, unsure why my instinct was to hide. I knew who it was. Four days earlier, I'd called Nat from Newport, his name and number listed on the back page of Lev's manual. The snow was probably still another month off, and Lev had sold me the two cords of firewood stacked in the garage, but it seemed a good idea to lay in the additional four cords I'd need to make it through the winter. Nat hadn't been home. I'd left a message with his son. "Any time would be fine," I said, trying to make a joke, "I'm not going anywhere."

The driver, his arm slung over the door of his truck, looked into the meadow with mild curiosity. Feeling foolish, I took a step out into the open. The truck slowed almost to a stop. The man, who could only be Nat, peered in my direction from under his baseball cap. I slipped back behind the tree. My heart was racing. The gnarled bark was cool to the touch. The leaves were a pattern of light and shadow. I couldn't help it. My instinct was to stay hidden. It was oddly thrilling, oddly advantageous, to be invisible. It wasn't a game. It felt primal. I slid my left eye to a gap in the dense tangle of apples and leaves. The man scanned the meadow once more, then drove on, down the steep grade towards the house.

A word of explanation. The idea of my morning walk was to walk as slowly as was humanly comfortable and to see and hear as much as I could see and hear. If the front door's glass pane glowed with sunlight, I'd step outside barefoot and wander up into the pasture. The apples were ready for eating, green flushed here and there with red, and marked with blemishes, like small patches of burlap. By the second week, I'd learned to choose not based on size or beauty—they weren't supermarket apples—but by ripeness, by how easily an apple gave itself to my hand. Most resisted, played coy, and I'd court them for days, the branch pulling back, the leaves rustling and chattering like so many protective sisters. The first bite was like walking outside all over again—the explosion of taste not like wading into the morning but like diving: the sunlight brighter, my skin more alive. If I ate slowly, it seemed I could taste the chill of fall nights, the warmth of late summer afternoons above the grasses. Then I'd continue on the thin trail of mud past the apple trees, past the old tiller on its side with rusting teeth, past the crumbling stone wall, and follow the trail as it began to climb. The forest was mostly maple and birch, with a high canopy that wasn't too dense, and about half a mile up, the dirt trail dissolved like a broken thought into nettles and fallen leaves. Here I had to go slowly if I was barefoot—the nettles stung so badly they left little red slashes on my calves—but the softness of the dirt was too pleasurable to pass up. I'd chart a path by looking up the hill to the space of sky where the trees opened. There was a shelf of land there, perched atop a steep meadow. A log cabin sat at the bottom whose owners must have lived far away—there was never smoke rising from the chimney—and beyond the valley the uninhabited hills rose again, leading out to a few distant peaks faint blue in the distance.

As I walked, I found myself trying to move through the woods without snapping any branches, with no sound beneath my feet. If my mind made any rustling sounds, I'd wait until it was quiet, too. There was no reason not to wait. Sometimes my mind would start back up, but I began to listen less and less. I didn't want to block myself from the morning in any way. And those first weeks, when I did manage to be slow and quiet, the woods made me feel as though I'd passed through a canvas, somehow passed through a curtain into the backstage of a painting, into the very source of its light. It was a realm where nothing could be translated. It was a realm I didn't want to come out of, a way of being I didn't want to leave. It felt like there was nothing I couldn't see. The first step back onto the soft dirt ruts leading down to the house often came tinged with a surprising sadness. The voice in my head, like a faithful dog, seemed to wait for me there.

So maybe that's why my instinct was to hide when I heard the truck coming. Being able to see so much made me feel like everything about me could be seen. A door that had opened to the day had also opened inside of me—and it wasn't a door you were supposed to leave open with other people.

"Wasn't sure if I saw you there," the man said, when I came down and joined him on the dirt outside the garage. "You was kind of like a deer in the fol-yage. There and not there."

His accent was a rustic version of the Kennedys'—*deer* more like *deahya*, *there* more like *theyah*. His skin had the papery look of old newspaper, a few age spots on his cheek. He was a few inches shorter than me. "Nat," he said.

We shook hands, and it felt like I was grasping an animal hide, my own hand suddenly soft as cotton. His shoulders looked sturdy beneath his jacket. "Real backwoods place here," he said looking behind him into the trees. "Nice."

I nodded.

"Always wondered what was at the end of this road."

Something in my body was still on edge, though he seemed to have already forgotten about my hiding in the meadow. I'd only been in solitude two weeks, but already I felt as alert as a wild animal. I was glad I didn't sniff him or suddenly go bounding off into the trees.

"I should put some shoes on," I said.

"Good idea. Wouldn't want to catch a splinter."

When I came back outside in my hiking boots, Nat had already begun unloading the wood from the truck, pitching log after log onto the ground. He seemed in no hurry—he stood on the flatbed, the wood piled higher than his waist, turning and pitching. As I climbed up on the truck and joined him, his pace stayed exactly the same.

"Nice day," he said.

"Nice day."

The logs were of varying width, roughly split, mostly beech, red maple, and yellow birch. I didn't know the maple from the beech, but Nat showed me the difference in the bark—the beech smooth, almost shaved looking, the maple rough and housing patches of moss in its ridges.

"Pretty simple to see," he said.

Easy for him to say. I knew birch from summers at camp, from using the little scrolls of papery white bark for kindling, but maples I could recognize only by their leaves, like the giant red one on the Canadian flag. Beyond that it just got worse. Oaks had acorns, pines had pinecones, and evergreens stayed green in winter. That was the grand sum of my arboreal knowledge. Studying the beech bark now, trying to picture a beech leaf on its stem, my mind felt like it was straining to sound out a word. *Was it oblong, did it have lines that looked like ribs?* I'd already grown proud that I knew the sun would rise every morning where the steep dirt tracks led down to the house, that it would set every evening in the hills beyond the weather-beaten deck. No information packet with a color-coded map, no guided tour given by an overeager voice walking backwards—my own slower kind of orientation was under way. But now I took a quick glance at the woods surrounding the house, and the hidden darkness under the trees daunted me. So many mysteries of bark and foliage, so many unseen realms of plants and insects. What had I been thinking, imagining there was nothing I couldn't see?

Nat flipped a log over with one hand, as though holding a large fish by the tail, and ran his finger along the grain of the wood. "Hardwoods burn hot," he said. "You'll stay nice and warm with these."

"They burn hot."

"Sure do."

Not wanting to look any more ignorant, I didn't ask why some wood might burn cool.

As we worked, I could hear a low wheeze in his chest. But he didn't bother resting. I wanted to say something, to suggest a break, but I didn't want to insult him. And I didn't want to look any more of a flatlander than I already did.

"Need help stacking?" he said when we were done.

I hesitated.

"Don't be a hero. I don't mind."

It was something I'd imagined doing myself, a small amends for having not chopped the wood—if I was a forest illiterate, the least I could do was earn my place here through a little physical labor. But Nat seemed more intent on exercising his vigor than I was on proving mine. And I suddenly didn't want to lose his company. In two weeks, I'd had no conversation that had lasted more than thirty seconds. With Tom Mooreland, who I had passed on his tractor on the farm down at the end of the dirt road, my instinct was to talk very little, to keep my distance. A part of me flickered with curiosity about his life—I wanted to know about the cows, the calves, how the milk was stored and shipped, how long his family had owned the farm, if he'd ever thought of living somewhere else. But I feared that if we talked too much, I'd begin to feel the farm down the road on my walks, which would lead me to feeling the road beyond the farm, and the interstate beyond that, and to everyone and everything I had left. But with Nat, the conversation seemed to pose no danger of moving beyond the forest. And it seemed important to absorb from him what I could—not by questions so much but by some osmosis of how he moved and looked and considered. He was at home here. This was country he knew.

We slid down off the truck and set to toting the logs into the airy coolness of the garage, stacking them waist high along the wall. Lev's two cords from the previous winter were intricately cobwebbed, and we worked on top of that. Nat's breathing riffled and purred beside me. My wool sweater quickly became a Rorschach test of clinging bark and sawdust, my fingers like a pin cushion for splinters.

"You know that trailer in the field, just down the road?"

I nodded.

"Yours truly. Not winterproof. But next summer I'll be there. Vacation place," he laughed, the wheeze coming back.

The trailer was maybe a half mile away, the closest one to the house. It sat alone, by two trees with golden apples, in the corner of wide field, a thin creek running alongside. I'd seen it on my weekly drive to the C&C. I liked that no one was ever there.

"My brother's got a camp up in Derby," he said. "All the way back in the woods. A place like this." He kept pitching as he spoke, the knock of log after log falling into place. "Got a nice platform, right close by. We wait up there for the deeyah."

"A platform?" I said.

"Up in an old oak. We just sit up there, bring a couple of beers, and wait with our bows."

I couldn't hide my amazement. "You hunt with a bow and arrow?"

"Bow hunting—more of a sport that way. Not too sporting sitting up there with a gun."

"Right," I said.

We kept moving from the sun of the driveway back into the cool shadow of the garage. Nat wasn't saying much, and I thought I'd finally lost credibility with him—maybe he was picturing me hunting with a pistol.

"I'd sure like a place like this," he said. "Nothing fancy but real backwoods. My wife don't like the idea of it. She told me so. But to be in the backwoods for a full season." He avoided my glance. "Not for the winter. That's a little crazy, pardon my French. Too much goddamned snow. A man could lose himself in all that." He coughed, spat something into a handkerchief he'd pulled from his back pocket. He examined his discharge briefly. "But I'd like it. I tell you that. If I could get it past the old lady. Maybe mud season till autumn. Just to see the changes, like the deeyah. Yes, sir. I'll tell my brother about this. Met a real backwoodsman today, I'll tell him."

The sunlight slanted into the garage from behind Nat, but I could see his face clearly enough. There was no trace of irony in his expression, no extra wink in his eye. I kept watching, but nothing in him changed as he pitched another two logs onto the stack. I wasn't sure whether he was putting me on or was just entirely sincere.

Eventually, the ground by the truck looked as though there had been a war between trees—bark carnage and wood dust everywhere. Nat said he'd be back in a few days with the next load. He shook my hand, glanced around once more, then climbed up into his Ford. He looked at me through the open window. "Good you're playing it safe. You'll have wood for next winter."

"Not sure if I'll be here next winter."

He secured his cap on his head, something surprisingly soft in the lines by his eyes. "You'll be here," he said.

The street moved as a blue-gray river, the houses slumbering boulders, the lights of Boston shimmering in the distance. My right eye was still swollen shut, and the world appeared vaporous, as though conjured by a spell. Stately brick Tudors hovered outside the car window, one with crenellated towers, another with stone lions posed out front, ferocious heralds of the suburbs. It was after two in the morning, and the trees draped everything in shadow, as though time itself had fallen asleep. But if I closed both eyes, there was the lean of the car, the gentle pressure to recline on the hills. The familiar sweep of the streetlights and the trees. My body enough to tell me where we were. My parents were taking me home.

Dad drove very slowly, as though the accident had yet to happen and could still be avoided. Mom's profile, drained and alert, looked washed out under the passing streetlights. Our family narrative had always been so straightforward. Mom and Dad had been high school sweethearts in the all-American city of Newburgh, New York. Dad's family didn't have any money, and he started working in a pocketbook factory at age thirteen, then paid his way through college by parking cars at a hotel in the Borscht Belt. Mom taught fourth grade outside Boston to help him pay for law school. Both Mom's sister and Dad's brother stayed in Newburgh, but Mom and Dad made the leap to Boston together, took the gamble together. And now Dad was a senior partner with a prestigious Boston firm, Mom worked as a career counselor, and their two sons were on their way. We were the American Dream. We were like the families on vacation brochures, just a little more Jewish. Dad with his twisted front tooth and slightly rakish smile, Mom with her short, stylish hair and lively blue eyes. The two sons tanned and athletic, horsing around in wholesome fun.

But now, in the hush inside the car, it was painfully clear the light on all of us had just gotten more intense. At our dinner table we didn't even talk about the other kind of family. A divorce of some friends might be mentioned, but quickly, quietly, *a shame, just awful*. And the skeletons in our own family closet— my father's father dying young, my aunt leaving college suddenly at the beginning of her senior year—were topics we never discussed. Dad would begin rearranging his silverware or repeatedly hitting the lock button in the car as soon as a conversation of this kind approached. "See what you've done," he'd said the night I'd finally asked Mom about her sister dropping out of college. "You've made your mother cry." The kitchen clock ticked above us. Mom wiped away her tears. I'd thought the conversation had been going well—Mom remembering how dinner after dinner, with her older sister home and there at the table, no one had said a word, how they pretended nothing had happened, and how she still didn't really know why her sister had come home. Mom seemed grateful for the chance to talk about it now, but Dad, mistaking her tears as being about her sister, rather than also being about their inability to talk about her sister, continued the tradition of shutting the conversation down. There was nothing more I could say. To push further would have been to threaten our tacit agreement about what we talked about and what we didn't. To run heedless through the family minefield. To question our very sense of who we were.

As Dad nosed the car down the driveway now, I felt a weakness through my chest, a fragile opening, like a long shut-up room was being aired. *How had I not prepared for this? How had I not known a collision was coming all along?* My breathing felt so quiet, as though I'd been caught at something, discovered with a secret I'd forgotten I was carrying. I'd been harboring a double life—one for everyone else and a different one for me. The one for everyone else was well trained at keeping people happy. He was slightly too independent for my parents' taste, but he was a son to be proud of—a Harvard student, a fine young man, one who looked like Bob Dylan circa 1964, before Dylan went electric. Probably a future lawyer. At worst a journalist. My strategy had been to play along—to be athletic but not a jock, smart but not a nerd, reserved but not aloof. To do nothing conspicuous, like a spy in one of those TV movies, the kind of guy who blends in so well he almost forgets he's a spy himself. And thanks to him, I didn't have to worry about the hidden part of me, the part that crept out while I was reading in my dorm room, the part whose sense of meaning came from something he couldn't articulate even to himself, the part who did well on tests because of what he daydreamed when he read, the part who played basketball because of the way it helped him travel in time. The part who wasn't a professional student, who didn't know how to please, who didn't really know anything. The part of me I'd never introduced to my family—because I'd never needed to.

But now it seemed there wouldn't be a choice. In the ER bathroom, after throwing up from the pain, I'd glanced up from the sink and hadn't recognized my own reflection. There was my familiar wavy brown hair, my familiar Nike t-shirt. But the face was a scarecrow version of my face: my eyelid swollen the size of a small plum, the skin so blue it was almost black, the eyelashes caked in blood. I hadn't wanted to move, hadn't wanted to break the illusion that the reflection wasn't me. It had happened to me before on crowded subway cars, in shop windows in Harvard Square—that split second of noticing a stranger's reflection in the window, of idly registering his hair or his mouth, and then another split second of realizing the stranger was me, the whole thing a minor existential carnival ride, complete with minor terror, minor thrill. But those other times I had filled back into my reflection instantly—like when a cloud passes and light pours back into a room. But in the ER bathroom, it was different. I didn't fill back in. And now, being ferried back to the room where I'd slept as a boy, I felt like I'd lost my reflection for good—my body turned inside out, the deeper part of me stirred up to the surface of my skin. I felt transparent, as though there was no way to hide anything.

The basketball hoop hung above the garage, the backboard ghostly in the glow of the outdoor light.

"Do you need help with anything?" Mom said, as the garage door descended jerkily behind us.

The garage smelled of dust, mildew, and rusted garden implements. I was still in my shorts and basketball sneakers, still holding my room keys and college ID. It felt like a bad dream: I was in the clothes for one place, but had been transported to another, a place that didn't look like itself. Mom and Dad didn't look like themselves. Mom's eyes had lost their usual wattage. Dad's face hung haggard in the garage light. Usually, when I came home, I had my backpack and a big duffel bag of laundry. Dad would greet me just inside the doorway with a hug—two firm pats on the back—then stand only a few inches away as I took off my shoes, unzipped my coat, as though he might learn about me simply by proximity. "Honey, give him some room," Mom would say, and, sheepishly, Dad would step away. Then Mom would speak in a kind of fanfare: "Everything, I want to hear everything." And in an overexcited little herd, we'd stumble into the kitchen.

But now my hands were empty. If there had been anything

for my parents to carry, I would have given it to them—just to weigh their worry down, to keep it from floating towards me.

"There's nothing," I said.

They waited.

I motioned for them to go ahead of me. I wanted no one behind me, nothing I couldn't see.

In late October, the rains came. The sky went dark, biblically dark, and for days the rain swept in sheets over the deck, pummeled the tar-paper roof, and pitted and puddled the dirt road. The maples went bare and slick. The birches grew rumpled looking, like crushed cigarettes after a party. There were no more leaves to make the rain shimmer and whisper rather than pound. The hills around the house thinned, opening into just a pencil sketch of themselves. There were fewer birds, fewer squirrels, fewer colors. The night's darkness got heavier, lasted longer. And maybe to fight my growing loneliness, my morning routine became a kind of ritual.

Dawn's blue-gray light would wake me, the leftover rain dripping from the eaves, my breath pluming visibly above the covers. I'd pull on my green wool sweater, my wool hat, creak down the steeply pitched stairs, the house gray and quiet with the windows to the woods. I'd put the battered kettle on, step into the bracing cold of the open garage, and fetch small branches from the scrap box. I'd come back inside and open the woodstove, kneel to sift through the lacy white ash for glowing embers, arrange the kindling, blow on the embers as though on a child's skinned knee, and return to the kitchen to pour the tea before the kettle began to whistle. Back to the garage for an armful of logs, another whiff of the wet woods, then back inside I'd kneel in front of the woodstove, lodging the logs over the growing flames. I'd adjust the grate on the stove to one slit, then sit down with the tea, which had now cooled enough to drink.

I took my time. The loneliness often felt as though the day was slow, and I was stuck outside that slowness, looking in. The way to feel less lonely was to slow down to the day's pace, to be inside it, and to look around from there. The clean, almost sharp waft of mint would cool behind my eyes. With each hot sip there was the complement of the wood smoke on my hands, as though I'd brewed the tea over a peat fire. Behind me, the wood popped, shifted, hissed. The warmth that had permeated the walls of the mug continued outward into my palms. Small tendrils of steam drifted into the air, just as my own breath had done as I gathered wood. I couldn't help feeling myself absorbing some of the tea's character—the way the strong mint scent made good on its steady promise, the way its taste didn't trail off on the tongue.

I can't say how long any of this took. Maybe ten minutes drinking the cup of tea, maybe longer. There was no clock in the house, no microwave numerals, no computer. No sense of time other than the daylight through the windows and my own sense of pattern—finding my hand on the kettle just as it began to tremble, or stepping outside to find the sun a white hole in the clouds above the highest spruce. There had always been clocks in classrooms, clocks on walls, clocks in public spaces—clocks like the digital one above Au Bon Pain in Harvard Square, or the famous clock tower in Piazza Maggiore, clocks as ubiquitous as the portraits in China of Chairman Mao or of Lenin in Russia. Not to mention the watches on nearly every wrist in Harvard Yard, nearly every wrist in Bologna, individual watches to make time's face resemble your own, while we were all joined by common time, the common progression, which we were assured of by the bells tolling at one church or another. There was undoubtedly something true about it—the light did come and go, the sun did rise and set, the moon did change its shape in the sky. And meanwhile we all got older. Time passed. I'd never given it much thought, but now it seemed bizarre that we'd managed to shrink something so profoundly primal and complex, something so near and so far, into little circular frames with numbers up to twelve. It was like we had domesticated the planetary motions, housed them in convenient cages, harnessed them as farm animals to help with our daily work. We needed them for lunch meetings. We needed them for parking meters. Every night, we slipped the turning of the Earth from our wrists. The few stars in Boston, I realized now, had been like worn-out horses back in their stalls. Their quiet snuffling in the dark, their unassuming beauty, so much greater than the use to which they'd been put. But here, the stars ran wild. With the overwhelming profusion of them, with the visible sweep of the Milky Way, it seemed there were more stars than sky. Time was everywhere. Not minutes and hours, not days and weeks, but seasons, centuries, millennia. Time was so much bigger in wild places. And feeling them reunited, time and space, I felt returned to some natural element, like a fish returned to water.

Before my accident, my preferred clock had always been other people. Hearing Matt flushing the toilet in the morning meant I needed to rouse myself for school; hearing footsteps pounding down the stairwell in Adams meant I was bound to miss breakfast; hearing the whir of the street cleaner on Via Irnerio meant Milena and I had only a few more hours before she had to steal back upstairs. But now my sense of time came only from the sun and the stars, and from the time it took for the water to boil, for the fire to catch. There were no other people, no other clocks. Maybe this was what pushed my morning towards feeling like a ritual—towards the sense that kindling the fire, making the tea, and even walking outside weren't just morning activities but a way of participating in something larger. Some community not of people but of the natural world. A community that might help me find my own resemblance to Time, my own rhythm as a part of its rhythm—an orientation beyond a face or a name.

Coming home from college always felt a bit like falling down the rabbit hole. Mom's unwitting attempt at organization, which often took the form of arranging tchotchkes, was to announce nearly every room's intended use. A red milk carton, suspended by a plastic stream of milk, hovered over a bowl of plastic cornflakes in the kitchen. A fluorescent orange arrow pointing down, painted by Mom herself, ran the length of the stairwell from the kitchen to the basement. In the downstairs bathroom, a small ceramic statue of a man in a bathtub sat at the edge of the bathtub. And the house's centerpiece was a McKnight print of a blue couch in a living room, which hung above the blue couch in our living room. As a boy, when no one was around, I'd steal across the Oriental rug, climb up on the blue couch, and wait to see if a little boy would appear on the couch in the painting.

But the morning after the accident, even my own room felt strange to me. Dust motes drifted in the sunlight above the radiator. The same posters of Larry Bird and Andre Agassi hung on the walls; the same National Latin Exam medals hung over the trophies on my bookcase. But the lines on the wallpaper seemed to be trying to hold the room in place. My bookcase, my desk, my chair—nothing was quite as solid as it was supposed to be. Every object looked like it had lost its outer coating. As though it had become a suggestion of itself, a mock-up for a rehearsal of some kind, until my real bedroom was ready to return. I'd always been especially proud of my trophies: the batters so dignified and balanced in their stances; the basketball players rising up effortlessly into jump shots; the gavel, for a debate tournament I'd won, poised at an angle as though it were rapping a bench for order. But now they just looked like trophies in a store window, with no substance behind them, no real victories holding them up.

I kept looking around my room, testing. My eyes still tracked together, and with any movement of my left eye, my right eye balked with pain. There was the swampy heaviness of the lid, the battered feeling of the eye itself, and that interior pain, no longer as piercing as a constant bee sting, but thicker, with a kind of dull vibration. The doctors had given me only Extra Strength Tylenol, which seemed like a very bad joke. *Didn't I at least get drugs?* On the other hand, no drugs meant the injury really couldn't be that bad. Two Tylenol sufficed for a hangover from too many Scorpion Bowls at the Hong Kong. Maybe the strangeness of my room was just a trauma jet lag, just the shock of everything that had happened and a bad night's sleep. The ER doctor had mentioned something about an adjustment period, the brain adapting in fascinating ways, but I hadn't really been listening. I wasn't interested in adjustments.

But as I emerged from my room and came to the top of the stairs, it was clear there wouldn't be a choice. I could see each stair clearly enough, but couldn't gauge the drop between them. There was just a series of lines, the distance between them getting smaller as they reached down to the foyer. They looked like a suggestion of stairs, a possibility of stairs, but nothing I could trust. I waited, like a skier at the top of an expert trail, trying to visualize my descent. It didn't matter how many times I'd taken the stairs not bothering to look. Matt, who was more than six feet tall by the time he was thirteen, had always been the one who had difficulty with the stairs, the one whose perpetual effort to catch up with his own body generally reminded me of how good I had it physically. But now the stairs looked treacherous, unfixed, fantastical. I gripped the wrought-iron banister.

My foot dangled. The plush blue carpeting received the ball, then the heel, the iron of the banister solid under my palm. It wasn't until my foot struck carpet that I knew for certain where the stair was, but the next stair was still in question. It didn't matter that memory and common sense told me each stair was the same distance down. My brain trusted my eyes—and my eyes said there was no telling where the next stair might be, no telling if I would step and not find anything solid, no telling if my foot wouldn't just keep falling, pulling the rest of my body down. I took another step, resting both feet on the same stair. I just needed to listen to my eyes less, to trust my other senses more. Appearance *was not* reality. I could almost feel my brain struggling to adapt. Vision no longer knew best. It could no longer be in charge.

Maybe this is what the Pakistani doctor meant when he'd explained to me that I'd lost binocular stereoscopy, the only means of perceiving depth. He said a normal person uses his eyes in concert: the disparity between the information his two eyes relay to his brain enabling him, by a kind of instant triangulation, to locate objects in space. Without the use of both eyes, a person can no longer perceive depth; he can only judge it with the help of depth cues, the same cues everyone uses instinctively: the size of known objects (bigger when closer), parallax (when you turn your head, objects farther away don't move as much), and occlusion (if an object is partially blocked, it's behind the object blocking it). So, the doctor explained, I would probably be able to manage in daily activities, especially as my brain adapted, but I still wouldn't *perceive* depth—I wouldn't have that clear sensation of space, of myself moving through a realm of dimensionality. This change, he said, could prove disorienting for some people.

And it was. Later that morning, I poured orange juice straight onto the kitchen table, pouring a good two inches in front of the glass. In the bathroom, there was no second bathroom behind my reflection, no space behind me, the whole room just a flat plane like a photograph. I kept wiping at an unsettling white spot on my nose—was it crust that had slid down from the crust sealing my eye?—before realizing the spot was just on the surface of the mirror, just a toothpaste stain. And out my bedroom window, while I was gazing at the Boston skyline trying to gather myself, a horribly enormous black bird blotted out the Hancock building. Its shape was monstrous. It was overtaking the entire tower. I stepped back, flinching. Then I saw. It was just a fly, crawling up the outside of the windowpane.

Mom and Dad were trying to adjust, too. My third night home, Dad asked at dinner if I wanted to consider pursuing the matter legally.

"Legally?"

"It's just an option. Something to consider."

"It wasn't Peter's fault."

Dad rested his fork on his plate. He looked like he hadn't been sleeping well. The pouches under his eyes were deeper than usual. "In a legal sense, fault might not be what you think it is. I'd give it some thought if I were you."

"It was an *accident*," I said.

"It's something to consider."

"It wasn't Peter's fault, Dad. It was no one's fault. It happened so fast."

"I put a call in to Neil Sugarman. He sends his best, by the way."

"It just happened. Things like this happen, Dad."

Mom gave Dad a look across the table and he fell quiet. The sounds of silverware continued. The meal went on. But the next night at dinner, he brought it up again. When I told him that I appreciated his offer, but there was nothing he could do, he looked stuck. Earlier that evening, when he'd come home from work, he'd given me a get-well card. On the front cover was a photograph of a hound dog wearing Coke-bottle-thick glasses, slumped at the edge of a porch. "Men of Thebes, look upon Oedipus," Dad's cramped handwriting began on the blank space inside the card. The quote, I knew, was from *Oedipus Rex*. We'd studied Sophocles my senior year at Roxbury Latin: Oedipus, unaware of his own identity, kills his father, has sex with his mother, then puts out his own eyes for shame. Dad, who wasn't very comfortable expressing his emotions, often relied on *Bartlett's Familiar Quotations* for important occasions. Maybe he'd thought that something from the classics, especially for his English-major son, would be appropriate. Maybe he had looked up *blindness*. The lines were the final haunting lesson of the play: "Though Oedipus towered up, most powerful of men, in the end ruin swept over him . . . let no man, in mankind's frailty, presume upon his good fortune, until he find life, at his death, a memory without pain." From "men of Thebes," I'd read the way a hungover man moves across a room, not wanting to start things spinning. I knew Dad hadn't read the play and couldn't have meant to imply that I deserved the accident. I knew, as his note at the bottom said, that he thought the quote was about vulnerability: "Sophocles' reminder of our vulnerability to mankind's frailties was exemplified in the starkest of terms this week by your accident. The bizarre and random nature of the event is almost unfathomable. I am so very proud to be your father." But I also knew nothing in our relationship had prepared us for this conversation—and a shared language wasn't going to suddenly form now, just because we needed one. The conspiratorial looks we exchanged watching the Celtics on TV, or as Mom launched into another non sequitur at dinner, were nowhere near sufficient for the task. The language we did share had been developed for the way life was, the way life had been.

Dad couldn't help me. And I couldn't help him to help me, as much as I wanted to.

"Well, just give it some thought. That's all I'm asking." He kept brushing imaginary crumbs from the table. He was a good poker player, but without cards in his hand he was easy to read. *Why was I blocking his effort to help me?* I changed the subject, told Mom the steak was delicious. She moved the conversation along. Dad was seated to my right, and when I leaned forward, he vanished in my peripheral vision. It was easier that way.

A few nights later, Peter called. Mom was cooking dinner, and I'd come downstairs for her company. Before dinner had always been one of my favorite times with her. As she dipped chicken in egg yolk or grated carrots for a salad, she existed in a spotlight of her own making, telling stories, making observations, until she couldn't remember where she'd started, and I'd have to run the conversation back for her like a court stenographer, having been trying the whole time to understand her by the gaps in between, by the jumps of her mind.

But now she wasn't talking. The whole week her face had been stricken with the look of a child with urgent news who has been told to keep quiet. For Mom, the world was made of stories. Stories about work, stories about that day's encounter at Star Market, and even the stories of strangers, which she'd ask about when she could—if a person looked even mildly approachable—and which she'd speculate on when she couldn't. "There's a story there," she'd say, as we left a restaurant or a store, a couple standing in silence. But now she didn't know what stories to tell or to whom. Years later, she'd admit the period after the accident was the one time in her life she avoided acquaintances at the market: she didn't want to have to answer questions.

So when Peter called, I seized the opportunity to shape the story myself. Mom was at the sink, grating carrots with deft flicks of her wrist. She was pretending not to listen to my conversation with Peter. And I was pretending, too. Because it wasn't really Peter I was talking to, it was her.

"I'm doing fine. The pain isn't bad. And listen, Peter, it was no one's fault. It could have happened to anyone."

The other end of the line got quiet. Mom's hand with the grater remained motionless at the sink. Her effort not to look at me was palpable.

"Freak accidents happen. And given that this was a freak accident, I'm lucky it wasn't worse. Not a car accident. You know, something like that. It wasn't your fault, Peter."

He asked when I would be back at school. My right eye was beginning to throb, as though it wanted to speak for itself. The pain had become less concentrated, less like a fist—but it felt like there was a part of me pressed up behind my eye, still trying to look out. I turned slightly away from Mom, towards the window. Keeping my voice level, I told him I'd be back at Adams House by Monday.

"Are you sure?"

"I'm sure."

"It's just, I talked to the House Tutor, and he said you could take exams after the summer. You don't have to rush it."

I turned farther towards the window. "It won't be rushing."

"You're sure? I mean, you looked, you know, pretty roughed up."

Anger was seeping through the cracks in my body. It felt like legions of spiders scurrying under my skin. An incitement to riot. Every shadowy, disaffected part of me was being summoned. All the roughnecks were emerging from their caves. They streamed through my blood with instant, built-in justification—they didn't come out for nothing.

I waited, looking out the window at the rhododendron. I couldn't let Mom see. I let the enormous purple flowers remind me of tennis season, of prom, of bumblebees. Mom couldn't tell Peter wasn't talking. I didn't care if the silence was making him squirm. Finally the militia retreated enough for me to stand my ground. "I feel good, Peter. I can read, I can study. Finals won't be any problem."

He began to say something, but I cut him off. I kept my voice slow. "Thank you so much for calling, Peter."

As I hung up the phone, Mom wiped at her eyes with the back of her wrist. A few carrot strips hung from her fingers. She held onto either side of the sink. "I don't know how you do it," she said.

She looked at me with a slowness that was rare for her. In it, there was respect, even surprise. The conversation had gone almost precisely as I wanted. But as I left the kitchen, I felt a strange lightness in my chest. I was not the son Mom was seeing. She believed I had a resiliency I did not have.

3

After the rains, they were everywhere—with their intricate, involute shells; their strange, long, wandering antennae. Large snails, small snails, the less glamorous, dark, houseless slugs. An invertebrate invasion. They inched along the rotting wooden beams in the long grass, along the edge of the dirt drive rutted and sheared by the rain's muddy flow, along the foot of the dilapidated shed. They left their glinting, silvery mucous trails on fallen leaves, on blades of grass—their runic bracelets of slime the only evidence they had actually moved. The slugs tended to group in tiny gangs of three or four, but the snails generally kept to themselves and could be anywhere. I began to admire them. They really were their own houses. I'd pass them in the morning on my walk, and, unlike the squirrels, they never scurried away.

One particularly raw afternoon, the rain calmed to a slanting drizzle, I went outside and squatted down in the grass. The sky was a wet newspaper, its headlines blurred; even the woodsmoke from the chimney smelled damp. The late fall afternoon had filled the house with a heaviness of waiting. The trees stood bare and forked out the windows, the snow had yet to fall. My daily rituals were what they were. Waking with dawn, tending the fire, making the slow walk up through the trees to the vista that looked out at the mountains. I was getting better at making no sound, better at spying squirrels before they spied me, better at not thinking. My senses were becoming more attuned, attaching me by so many silken threads to the morning light, to the subtle changes in the air, to the movements of the wind and the rain. The echoes of Boston were fading, as though the weeks were miles, as though I was getting farther away. I still had pangs for conversation, especially at night after dinner, but they were becoming less painful, less of an accusation, and more just nostalgia for a different way of life. So much of loneliness, I realized, was social envy, the desire to be included, but with no prospect of being included, that layer of loneliness sifted away. Solitude wasn't so bad, I told myself. But I also knew these late fall days were a kind of minor league, just preparation for the winter. The squirrels were preparing, thrashing through the leaves and gathering acorns; the trees were preparing, scattering their last leaves to the wind; and I needed to be preparing, too. Not just with a cupboard full of Ramen noodles and wood stacked shoulder high in the garage, but with something else. Patience, maybe. A deeper kind of attention that might endure when there was little but snow to see.

Which is probably what sent me outside to sit with the snails. The desire to practice, to prepare for winter's slowness. And the desire to see more—to keep getting closer to something that was real. Or maybe it was just the need for company. The need to be in the same place with another creature, to not be so alone with the barren trees. I assumed my loneliness wouldn't feel so raw once the snow fell, but I didn't like waiting.

Towards the top of the yard, slouching along by the moss at the edge of the birches, I found one. It was dainty. Small and lacquered brown, its blue-grayish body lightly stippled on either side of its shell. Its antennae probed haphazardly, like hands in the dark. When I waved my own hand overhead, they retracted with surprising speed. Two crows drifted by, their wing beats loud and papery. The rain soaked entirely through the seat of my jeans. The antennae reemerged. The snail began to move. Or did it? It seemed headed towards a patch of nearby moss, but who could tell at this speed? I left off studying its shell, the

bending of the grass, the painfully slow emission of slime. My
only effort was to keep an open gaze, the way I imagined the
snail did, absorbing whatever offered itself to my eye. I lasted
maybe fifteen seconds. There was so little to see. I tried again.
But the snail was *barely* moving. And I kept hitting some barrier—like the day, or just my brain, wouldn't let me drop below
a certain speed of seeing.

As I tramped back down to the house, annoyed with myself,
as though I had failed our first date, I remembered something
from my Psych 1 class in college. We'd read about studies that
showed that sighted people have all kinds of blindness. When
subjects were flashed an image of an airplane without wings
aloft in the sky, they would respond that the plane had wings;
when shown a gorilla running through the middle of a basketball game, they would respond that there'd been no gorilla.
Even more amazing, when an experimenter ducked behind a
desk—in a show of looking for papers—and a different experimenter stood up in his place, subjects didn't notice that the person had changed. Not only did their brains fill in the wings,
remove the gorilla, and see the new experimenter as being the
same as the old, but they also had no doubt they knew exactly
what they had seen. I'd loved reading about those studies senior
year, loved knowing that people were missing out on a hard and
fast reality, just as I was. Everyone's reality was a construction of
their brain. Sometimes I even thought I saw more than most
people, simply because I'd become aware there was so much I
wasn't seeing. If everyone's reality included blind spots, if that
was simply the nature of perception, and my own perception
was constantly being reminded of its blind spots, wasn't I seeing
a little more than most? It was a comfort to think I hadn't only
lost something—to think I'd been given a way of seeing, or not
seeing, that was potentially profound, if only I could figure out
how to use it.

But remembering all this didn't help with the snails. Day after day, soggy pants after soggy pants, I tromped up into the grass to try again. I didn't just want to be aware of what I wasn't seeing—I wanted to *see more*. To be aware of the gaps, the blind spots, and to see into them. But I wasn't getting very far. I could last about five minutes without wavering from a kind of smooth attention, then maybe seven minutes, maybe even ten. But at some point I always hit a wall. My mind would start to wander. I'd think about lunch or about the wind. The snail would be probing away as patiently as ever. I'd rejoin him for a few minutes, but my focus would drift off again. I couldn't stay with him, couldn't keep pace with the slowness. The snail kept beating me. And I found myself getting frustrated, feeling the size of my foot as I stood up, the angry speed waiting in my legs.

One chill morning, the sun sliding out and silvering the puddles in the road, I decided to go for a bike ride, only my second since I'd moved in. Snow wasn't too far off, and I wanted to get a little exercise while I could, to feel myself moving. The muddy ruts wound past the meadow, straightened alongside the open field, and faded in the slow rolls beneath the canopy of branches. With each sharp wind, the branches let loose brief, shimmering showers, like a woman shaking out her hair. It was good to be propelling myself forward, good to smell the ferns and the wet rocks, good to feel my blood moving in my veins. I'd grown so accustomed to walking speed that now riding speed felt wildly fast. The wet dirt sucked at the tires, a thin spray of mud pinwheeled up onto my hands. I felt like I was absorbing the world with my face. I pedaled faster, picking up speed on the downhill slope, when up ahead, right in the middle of the road, between two muddy puddles, I saw the largest snail I'd ever seen. Its shell had to be the size of my fist. Its body stretched out on either side of it. It was right in the middle of the road, right in the middle of my path. My speed felt so good. I knew I should

turn the handlebars, but my hands were not turning the handlebars. The signal from my brain was growing weaker. My body
was growing in strength. My leg muscles were singing and I
pedaled harder. I crushed the snail's shell with the front tire and
crushed it again with the back. The crackling was loud and
thrilling. Blood rushed to my face as I sped up the far side of
the rise. I felt fast, cruel, powerful. Guilty and relieved. I felt
human.

Slowness kills, a voice in my head said. And I laughed horribly.

Going to class, studying, even finding my jeans balled up on the
floor exactly where I'd left them—everything about being back
at college was a relief, as though time had stopped for a week,
my life waiting to be filled back in. There were exams to study
for, papers to write. And reading and writing, more than anything else in my life, felt as they always had.

My third night back, Andrew threw me a "welcome back"
party. No music, a few beers, the mood subdued. Conversations
sparked and waned around the room about upcoming exams,
summer jobs—all of it more quiet than usual, as though we were
in an open field where a storm might suddenly arise and compromise plans. But the not-talking about my eye was a comfort,
the accident's simple presence in the room enough. Early in the
party, I had offered the basic information—optic nerve severed,
no surgery required, glad to be back—but just like a press con-
ference, just to have the news out, so I wouldn't have to deliver
it again. There didn't seem much else to say. Really, what I
wanted everyone to believe was the same story I wanted Mom
to believe, which was the same story I wanted to believe myself.
*I'd dodged a bullet. It was a freak accident that could have been life-
altering, but I got lucky.*

Each of my friends looked so young, so clear, so alive. There was Ray, with his easy, handsome California face, but so earnest, so methodical when he approached me, as though he'd rehearsed his comments in advance. And there was Alexis, the moody heartthrob of our bunch, standing sideways, looking out at the room as though everything had already been said, as though we were onto the same truths. His dark curly hair and dark eyes made him look like a movie version of a Dostoyevsky character—deeply thoughtful, mildly tormented, but too pretty to be intimidating.

Andrew, who had been shifting foot to foot in his black jeans, handed me the May issue of *Tennis*.

"Thank you," I said.

"Don't worry about it." His eyes were everywhere but on mine. "Good article on the second serve," he said.

The doctor had said I wasn't allowed any sports, not for at least three months, not until the blood behind my eye dissipated. "I appreciate it," I said.

Andrew kept staring at the floor. Usually, he was the first into any conversation. At dinner, if someone was telling a story he'd already heard, his lips would involuntarily start mouthing the words as he listened, as though the story were his as well. He was the best athlete in our class, but he was really a literary cheerleader at heart. He'd barge into our room, book in hand, and declare, "You have to read this Carver story, it's fucking awesome!" Or, "Seamus Heaney is a goddamned legend!" On court he'd grow indignant if his opponent dared to believe in any chance of victory, but off court he was more open and curious than anyone I'd ever met, but his confidence needed to be filled in by his friends—his love for that Carver story or Heaney poem not complete until he'd succeeded in recruiting your excitement, too. He was the perfect friend for me—his enthusiasms pulling me into long literary conversations, his status as an athletic stud making those conversations safe.

But I didn't know what to say to him now. Maybe he needed me still to be something of an athlete—or, being a friend, maybe he just knew I might still need to feel that way myself. But the feeling I had, the extra space in the air, was like that odd quiet after a funeral—that sense that the world is held together much less firmly than you think. And I had no idea how to say any of this, at least not in any way that was simple, that went along with the story about myself I wanted to believe.

As Andrew moved into another conversation, I knew no one would come any closer. And the hum of the party, the easy warmth of companionship—it was almost enough. It reminded me of the car ride back to college. The May greenery of Hammond Pond Parkway had streamed by outside the window, the trees appearing both looser and more dazzling than they ever had. It was easier now to see shape, to see pattern—and much harder to see the leaves, dappled by the sunlight, as solid, as limited to just being leaves. My vision see-sawed between the two—if I leaned into the world and kept a hard focus, the leaves looked as they always had, though a bit more flat; if I leaned back and let my focus go soft, the leaves transformed into shimmering patterns, the spaces between them filled with light, each tree like some primeval chandelier. The game scared me a bit, how easy it was to lose the firmness of the world, its definition— to feel, as with the very word *definition*, how much meaning depends on shape. But the game also relaxed me, which was enough for me not to question it too much. And now I found I could do the same thing with my friends, could see them and myself as patterns of conversation, patterns of silence. What came naturally visually, apparently, also came naturally psychologically. But there was a sadness in the center, some heightened sense of the space I'd always felt between me and other people. Being a confidant was a role I liked, listening to Mom in the kitchen before dinner, or to Andrew raving about some new poem, but it wasn't a role I'd ever learned to let someone play for me. My privacy had always been a natural moat, a helpful protection. But it was strange. Now that I felt most vulnerable, it was a moat I did not entirely want.

The snow began. It spit, it blew, but it kept falling. It fell, and fell, and I began to forget the air between the trees wasn't always filled with snow, that the windows had ever showed stillness or sky. Inside the woods the air grew quieter, more intimate. The snow took no notice. It fell through the gray, flat afternoons, and it fell, brushing against the windowpane above the futon, through the starless night.

Nothing was more simple and more complex than walking outside in the morning. At first, there was everything and nothing, too much and too little: too much space and brightness and sky, too little that was legible in any language that was human. The shocking brightness of the snow, the cold on the exposed skin around my eyes, the scent of the woodsmoke pushing in behind the chill, which offered a kind of balance and kept my perspective from contracting in the cold. My footprints of the day before would be gone. I would stand there in the trackless white, in my black snowboots and snowpants, breathing in and out heavily behind my neckwarmer, like a man newly arrived on the moon. I would wait to see movement, to hear movement. The ragged dance of the smoke from the chimney against the bright blue sky. Or a parcel of snow sliding from the overloaded arms of one of the evergreens. And the dull percussion of snow hitting snow, the mild reflex of the branch swinging toward its place again, would include me, like the opening of a conversation, a first word. Not the first thing to move, I would feel safe to begin moving—as though I had been welcomed, as though I wasn't intruding into a conversation in which I had no part.

I kept my snowshoes and poles up by the car, at the top of

the steep pitch beside the meadow. By mid-December, the snow was already two feet deep, and every morning I'd strap in to one shoe, then the other, and tromp like an ungainly prehistoric creature towards the trees. There was no sound but the rustle of my jacket and the mild, plush sinking of the snowshoes into the snow. The apple trees glimmered. The abandoned tiller poked a few softened, curious teeth above the snow, like the periscope of a strange submarine. At the entrance to the trail, past the buried stone wall, a lone hemlock seemed to stand sentry. To duck under its snow-feathered branch and push into the woods felt like going inside a warmly lit room—there was the sense of being safely held, of being somewhere that surrounded and contained me. The quiet was different under the trees.

The path rose as a smooth white avenue. Occasionally, my tracks from the day before were still there, the twin trough of the snowshoes and the alternating pockmarks of the poles, and sometimes they were crossed by the hieroglyphic tracks of a squirrel or deer or snowshoe hare, as though in some other realm a friendly meeting had occurred, forest gossip exchanged. As I pushed upward, I'd pause to listen every so often below the brushing of my jacket, below the tufted sound of my snowshoes, until my hearing touched ground with the silence. A dim humming, like a steady rush of water far away. It seemed to open a pocket in time, to open the years. Decades, even centuries, were able to slide through. The more western forests of Vermont had been clear-cut for timber after the Civil War (and reforested later), but not being near any large rivers for transport, the forests of the Northeast Kingdom had gone largely untouched. I'd read in one of Lev's guidebooks that glaciers, with sheets of ice more than a mile deep, had pushed through this land thousands of years ago, carving the hills and mountains, depositing boulders and rocks as they went. It was the same land I was standing on. The birch and pine and maple were the same. The wind was the same, and the snow and the sky. The silence wasn't just the silence of the moment. It gave me a sense of carrying something in myself that was the same, too, something delicate but abiding—something that had remained no matter the radical changes in my life. Something essential I might grow closer to, especially as my outer layers fell away.

Up where the maples stopped, at the vista overlooking the far hills rising into the mountains, I'd drive my poles into the snow. I'd unstrap my snowshoes and lie back, arms at my side. The pounding of my heart would gradually subside, my chest rising and falling, rising and falling. I'd feel myself sinking into the coldness of the snow, into the quiet. The snow below me would gradually warm with the heat moving through my legs, through my arms, and the sense of my body would grow quiet, until I wasn't thinking about the cold at all, as though my body had become a door that was open, the quiet of the hillside coming in and filling me in some way that kept me warm. It didn't feel like I was floating or falling but only like there was nowhere to float or fall. I could stay this way for some time.

Eventually, when I sat up, the hills and distant mountains looked different. The land felt oceanic, unimpeded in all directions. The frosted trees on the hills seemed to continue forever, well beyond what the eye could see, and the bluish, snow-capped mountains looked both very close and very far. The ease in the land's movement, the way no part of it seemed divided from any other, accorded with the way I felt—with the way I saw. There was an organization to the land but with a wide margin, with no precise division of space, with no need of my hand or foot to turn any line solid. I felt at home, in a habitat that fit with my senses, as though some membrane had been dissolved. I was back in the world rather than outside it. And seeing this way felt like a kind of cleansing, an absolution, as though the land itself had opened to take me in.

———

This wasn't a good sign. I tried to blink it away, to look again, but nothing changed. Exam period had begun, and I was sitting on my bed in Adams House, my Riverside Shakespeare heavy as a small dog on my lap. A chair had scraped along the hardwood floor in the room above me and I'd looked up from reading *King Lear.* After a bit more scraping, the sound had stopped. But something was wrong with my ceiling. There was a shadow where the ceiling ended, and a hovering where the brown wood molding began. I waited for the shadow to go away, for my normal sense of space to return. But it didn't return. No matter if I stared harder, no matter if I turned my head. The lines of the brown molding had a phantom-like quality, a margin for error. As though my ceiling didn't begin in any one place, as though the plaster and the wood molding were no longer solid. It was easy to picture how I had seen the ceiling before—how sharp the division between the molding and the ceiling, how definite my sense of depth and space. But that configuration of lines, which had been tied in place as neatly as a present, had come untied. Geometry had gone off-duty. My ceiling's *formality*, in both senses of the word, was gone. I couldn't tell with any certainty where my ceiling began.

In my two weeks back at school, I thought I'd already made all the necessary adjustments. Instinctively, I sat in the last row in crowded lectures, generally on the right-hand side, to have the whole lecture hall in front of me on my left. I walked up to class later than usual, so as not to be caught in the crush of so many bodies on the sidewalk. On rainy days, I trailed a little behind Alexis, Ray, and Andrew—without sunlight there were fewer shadows, fewer depth cues, and it was the best way to avoid the sharp spokes of umbrellas, menacingly poised at eye level, and also not to miss a curb. No one really seemed to notice. Finals were coming up, the rush of the semester was at its peak. Especially once my eye healed outwardly and the blood inside it went away, my friends tended to forget—probably because they couldn't *see* that anything was different. The Pakistani doctor had been right. He'd told me my eyes would move normally, would continue to "look" at the world just the same. The metaphor he'd used was a toaster oven with a broken cord: the toaster looks fine, it just can't be plugged in. Which led to some strange situations. About a week after my return, a classmate came trotting towards me on the grass in front of Lamont. He was out of breath, and looking at me a bit too closely. "I heard the most horrible story," he said. "I'm so glad to see it isn't true."

"What story?"

"Some of the guys said you lost an eye playing basketball. That it actually came out of your skull. That it was rolling around on the court."

I told him what happened. I explained about the optic nerve.

"No shit. No shit! You mean, you don't see anything out of that eye? Which eye? This one?"

He held his finger in front of my face, wagged it back and forth. He was peering at me like a lab specimen. I had the feeling he was seeing one version of me, while another version was looking out at him. It felt like a trench inside me, like there was an actual space of about a foot between where he saw me and where I was seeing him from. Gently, I had put my hand around his hand and pulled it down to his side.

But the only place I was having any real physical difficulty was the dining hall. The juice machine, which was situated by the doorway to the tables, posed a particular hazard. After filling two glasses, I'd turn to the right with my full tray to go out to the tables, but someone who hadn't been there a moment before would suddenly materialize on my right and we'd crash. I crashed into a sophomore from Kansas who reminded me of

Woodstock from the *Peanuts* gang, her collarbone exceedingly frail as we bent down to the floor. I crashed into Steve Martins, the hockey stud, who barely noticed me bouncing off him. I even crashed into Prokopow, the house tutor who had suggested I stay home and postpone exams until fall. Each time, there was nothing to do but apologize, clean up the ruined food, and be angry with myself. *Why couldn't I remember I'd lost peripheral vision on my right-hand side? How had I forgotten that space immediately to my right existed?* My brain somehow hadn't registered, no matter the frequency of my crashes, that my blind spot had expanded. The missing area in my brain's map was like the inverse of a phantom limb—instead of my brain filling in a hand or arm that no longer existed, it had subtracted the awareness of a physical space that *did* exist. The worst part of which wasn't the humiliation but the impossibility of an honest apology. I *looked* normal. I couldn't tell the story every time I crashed, couldn't just crash into people with my story, too. The story felt too emotional, too strange to put into words. Or maybe I could have tried, but my instinct was just the opposite—to keep my blindness invisible. But I couldn't help wondering, as I returned to the line for a replacement helping of Tater Tots, how many other people lived with this kind of doubleness. I'd look at the faces above the salad bar, faces strangely vulnerable as they moved along with their blue trays. *How many of them also felt a divide? How many of them looked one way but felt entirely another?*

I didn't want to think about it too much. No reason to get all philosophical. Apart from my crashes, my physical adjustments really had been going well. I was acclimating to the various sets of stairs, like the smooth gray, unevenly worn ones in my entryway: step higher than necessary, then let your foot, coming down, locate the stair. The same tactic worked with shaking hands: keep reaching until contact. Not too much had to be different, I told myself. Already my hearing was adapting, listening not just for sounds but for *space*—the rhythmic scuffing of footsteps behind or beside me or the wind rush of cars coming down Mass. Ave. This happened without any effort on my part, just a sympathetic response, as the doctors called it, as though my ears were actually *sympathetic* and showing a kind of moral support to my eyes. My Spidey Sense was what I called it. I'd know Andrew was about to appear in my bedroom's doorway—maybe from a subtle shift of air currents on my face or maybe from the creaking of the floorboards. I didn't even know *how* I knew. It was a little spooky. Apparently, studies show that the visual area of the brain begins to process auditory and tactile information within five days of the loss of vision. The occipital cortex just automatically starts using the way sound travels through space, and the touch of wind patterns on your skin, to help you *see*, to help orient you spatially in your surroundings.

All of which had been fine, just some neurological redecorating, something that didn't require too much thought. But now my ceiling wasn't in any particular place. The light coming through the windows was just simple late-day light, but the air around me felt different. My heavy wooden bureau looked weightless, permeable, as though I could put my hand through it. The more I looked out from the solid island of my bed, the more my room felt as though gravity had been altered, as though every object hovered rather than sat. It seemed my vision couldn't help but tread lightly, as though it were waiting for some more definite confirmation of what I saw. As though, like Gloucester in *King Lear*, I needed to learn to "see feelingly," to see not so much with eyes but with my hands and with my heart.

This wasn't so different from how my bedroom had felt the morning after the accident, but this wasn't the morning after. Life was supposed to have returned to normal. Finals were just a few days away. But my ceiling wasn't coming back. I felt betrayed, like when you look into the sky for a plane after hearing its sound, then have to find the plane with your eyes farther along in the sky—some gap suddenly there between reality and your sense of reality. But then usually your brain, working like a minor god, just moves the airplane's sound to match the airplane's location in the sky. Your hearing and vision align, like two competing mirrors sliding into one, and that gap vanishes. The plane is where it is, which means you are where you are. But now the gap wasn't going away. I was stuck in it, stuck in a strange, steady awareness that my sense of reality was assembled by a team, a team not even close to perfect. This wasn't a well-turned couplet in Shakespeare. It wasn't even a secret passageway at the back of a wardrobe or a long curious tumble down a rabbit hole. And I wasn't sure whether I was one step further away from reality or one step closer to it—because that depended on what reality really was.

In a way, I'd always lived between worlds—between the jocks and the nerds, between my parents' interests and my own, and I'd understood myself as the ever-shifting but broadly consistent sum of those gaps. But this gap had always been the one that felt too wide: the gap between what I saw with my eyes open and what I saw with them closed. How strange it had always felt to stand from my bed after reading a poem I pictured in my mind—the snow, the quiet, the woman waiting and not waiting for her lover—and to walk outside into the Cambridge afternoon where I saw less vividly, and, it seemed, needed to see less vividly to get where I was going, to do what I needed to do. But now those two distinct realms—behind my eyes and outside them—had drifted so close as to become almost indistinguishable. The ceiling, the molding, the walls: they were all suddenly like something out of a fairy tale where a spell has been cast, where a threshold has been crossed. The entire physical world suddenly seemed a doorway into possibility. I liked it and didn't like it. It felt like an initiation, but an initiation into a realm where I wasn't supposed to be.

I got up from the bed, dragged my black desk chair to the wall. Even standing two feet off the ground, I couldn't tell exactly where the molding ended. The ceiling was still too high to touch. The doctors had warned me about the blood behind my eye, close to my brain. I knew, given my persistent headaches, that jumping from the chair wasn't the best idea. But I needed to know, as well as I could, where my ceiling began.

And so I jumped.

4

The news from breakfast wasn't good. In the cupboard above the stove, there were two more packages of Ramen noodles, one package of spaghetti, but no sauce, no cereal, no bread, no peanut butter. In the refrigerator, no milk—just the crusty dregs of some blackberry jam and Lev's sad yellow box of baking soda. I could go a few more days, maybe even a week. I could rifle through the dusty canned goods in the bomb shelter. But sooner rather than later I needed to get to town. I needed to get food.

The snow was only about a foot deep, but drifts had formed alongside the open field, deep wind-carved cornices that looked like white-capping waves. This morning, even with the fire built up and throwing heat, the chill off the front door was shocking. Generally, as a point of pride, I avoided looking at the thermometer affixed to the side of the house, preferring to take in the weather for myself. Snow squeaking underfoot meant cold; instant nostril hair freezing meant very cold; and for more nuanced readings, there was the sharpness of the air on the exposed skin by my eyes and how far up into the woods my toes went numb. The thermometer's precision had come to seem superfluous—a stand-in for my own body, which was less finely calibrated than the thermometer's little black lines, but told me more: the direction of the wind, the smell of coming snow, the idiocy of not wearing wool socks. My body was probably even sending my brain news updates I didn't know it was receiving— teams of meteorologists and first responders shuttling around, all of it simply registering as an instinct to turn back towards the house or to snowshoe deeper into the woods. But this morning, with my brain actually piping up and telling me I needed to get to town, I checked the circular thermometer. The long red arrow had keeled over and given up. The numbers to the right of zero stood aimless, overly ambitious, like the speedometer of a car up on blocks. Everything, including the very possibility of temperature, canceled on account of the cold.

After the first snow two weeks earlier, Nat had magically appeared in his truck, a battered yellow plow angled rakishly on the front. We hadn't spoken since his final wood delivery in October, and I was planning on calling him but didn't want to call until the road was truly impassable and the cupboard truly bare—not just because of my backwoodsman pride but also because of my backwoodsman lack of money. But with only about six inches on the ground, he'd come on his own. He'd rolled down his window, ashed his cigarette. "Long stretch coming in *heayah* from Mooreland Road."

It was a very long stretch.

"I'll show with the snow. Not for a few inches like this, but when you need it."

He'd looked straight ahead, the truck idling. I tried to think of what I could afford. I had just under $1,900 in my bank account. The wood was paid for, no expenses other than about a $150 a month for food, but Lev had mentioned the possibility of staying for another year.

Nat suggested $225 for the winter. I couldn't tell if he was lowballing, so the flatlander would do his negotiating for him, or if he was just being generous. Did I look that hard-up?

"Deal," I said.

Since then, there'd been a few inches almost every night, and he hadn't come. But I didn't want to call. I didn't want to look helpless or desperate. I didn't want to look like some young idealist who had gotten himself in over his head. And, on a deeper level, maybe I needed to believe that Nat really was looking out for me—and that if the snow warranted it, he would come.

But now I needed food, something with color. I'd dreamed of orange juice. The orange radiance of it, its impertinence against the dim, gray sky. Then just one swallow. And a circus starting up inside my face—the tartness a trapeze act in my cheeks, the sugar a strapping majorette prancing in my throat.

So I trudged up to the car. The steering wheel was bone-cold through my gloves. I let the engine run for a good fifteen minutes, but the car still felt like it was a part of the snow and shouldn't be disturbed. Eventually, I downshifted into the lowest gear and rolled towards the open field. Alongside the apple trees, there were no drifts, just a silent whiteness gliding beneath the car. The motion felt so smooth, an entirely new mode of transport. The first challenge was the sudden rise, at the curve before the road straightened out alongside the field. Spindrift was blowing in sheets off the top of what looked to be a three-foot drift. I hit the gas. My little white Honda acted like a motorboat, the undercarriage bouncing off the snow, white plumes spraying to the side, the car rocking and pulsing, snow flashing up over the windshield. My foot held steady. I couldn't see, but the car was fighting for momentum, the steering wheel resisting my hands, the car angling towards the trees. I let up on the gas, and the car lost traction, juddering to a stop. The thick snowy branches hung over the hood, as though beckoning. The quiet held the car like a glove. My stomach growled and I thought of the empty refrigerator, how hungry I would be. I shifted into reverse and the wheels spun. The sound was terrible—no better than a toy car with its wheels in the air. I got out with the shovel. Good Lord, it was cold! The air felt like a thin layer of ice cracking and spiderwebbing around my face. I shoveled until my hands were numb. Got back in the car, hit the gas.

Stuck again. Reverse ten yards. Hit the gas, stuck again. I felt like an old-style football team: three yards and cloud of dust, only there was more snot running out of my nose.

There was just too much snow. And no getting out.

Two days later, Nat came. As I trudged down past the buried stone wall and into the meadow at the end of my morning walk, I could hear a truck in the distance. It was a bright, cloudless day, and with no leaves in the trees the engine sound seemed to be coming from all directions at once. I'd taken another inventory of the cupboards and had been limiting myself to two meals a day. Breakfast that morning had been some cooked pasta with the old blackberry jam. If two more days passed, I'd told myself, I would give in and call.

I leaned against my poles, listened, and as the picture from my ears filled into the shape of Nat's truck, with a real yellow plow and the real Nat behind the wheel, I felt a rush of gratitude so deep it shamed me. Nothing came out of my mouth, but my body felt like it was emitting a sound as I stood there—like music was broadcasting from inside me out into the winter air. It was too intense. I didn't want to need anyone this badly. I hadn't felt particularly lonely before hearing his engine, but it disturbed me how happy I was to hear him—not just to know the road would be open but to know he hadn't forgotten me. I *existed* for him. This house in the woods, with me inside it, *existed*. I didn't like thinking about my parents thinking about me, worrying about my sanity, or even about Ray imagining me like some modern Thoreau, living deliberately beneath the pines, or about Andrew calling me a woodsman Bob Dylan—*how does it feel, to be on your own, with no direction home*—because those conceptions of me, however generous, didn't really match up with how I felt. But for Nat to remember me was reassuring. His conception of me, whatever it was, didn't start with my old life.

As I snowshoed through the meadow towards the road, he raised one finger from his steering wheel in salute, his cigarette dangling from his mouth. I wanted to say hello, to talk about the weather, to talk about anything, to bring him his money. But he ignored me, the truck shunting forward and back, tires spinning and then catching, the plow battering the soft snow into solid banks. There was music playing from his radio—something country, something with strings. To get his attention required yelling, but I couldn't bring myself to do it. My voice had been dormant for too long. Sometimes at dinner, just opening my mouth for the first spoonful of soup, my jaw would ache from disuse. And the quiet around me was too large; too much would fall clattering around me if it shattered. So I started towards him on my snowshoes, sliding down the snowbank by my car. But he didn't see me. When he did, and I raised my hand, he just raised one finger again, and the truck sped out of the meadow, little chains of snow spitting up from the back tires as he went.

The road was clear now. The track led all the way to the grade that led down to the house. I should have been relieved, should have been rejoicing, but as my snowshoes clomped onto the hard empty road, I had the strangest feeling. A physical disappointment, an awful lightness in my hands and feet. Unformed words clustered in my throat—they had no reason to take shape now. They were stillborn, caught in the long delivery between me and the outside world. I could feel them slowly sinking back down into the depths. The most painful part wasn't the words themselves but all that they were swimming through— that distance between my silence and how it might feel to talk to another person. I'd had no idea the distance had grown so large.

After the accident, perhaps on the advice of her doctor friends, Mom had suggested I see a therapist. Every month or so, she'd bring it up again on the phone, and I'd tell her there was no need, perhaps *she* should see a therapist, everything was fine. But fall of senior year, with everyone planning for the future, I wondered if she hadn't been on to something.

Preparations were being made. Futures were being plotted. It was only November, but you couldn't walk into Adams House and not feel it. Every meal had the diffuse buzz of Grand Central Station—harried seniors checking for posted maps, for spinning placards, for the time on some enormous clock. Hardly a day passed that someone didn't interrupt a conversation about cute sophomore girls or Karl Marx to hurry off from breakfast in a blue suit, hair combed, a leather folder at his side. Representatives from Goldman Sachs, Morgan Stanley, and McKinsey were on campus to recruit. Everyone was herding towards the future. Even the frighteningly studious kids who seemed to come from nowhere, who emerged from the Widener stacks maybe once a semester for hygiene purposes only, were suddenly passing through the dining hall in high heels and makeup, with new blouses and haircuts, their backpacks on over their new outfits, little corporate butterflies not quite emerged from the chrysalis.

My friends were staying relatively calm. Ray and Alexis grudgingly filled out med school applications despite respective fantasies of writing and filmmaking. Meanwhile, Andrew was training for the minor leagues of pro tennis, standing shirtless in front of our window at night, studying his reflection in the darkened glass as he mimed service returns. He'd practice his hip turn, practice it again. His image hovered in the leaves of the oak outside the window, as he hit imaginary ball after imaginary ball into the unknown.

We were all trying to do the same in our minds—imagining possible futures, trying to glimpse how we might look in one scenario or another. This was 1994. America looked to be entering a golden age, one even more golden because it was ready to include us—no more Cold War, democracy victorious, organizations like Teach For America and AmeriCorps popping up to address social issues, rock stars like Bruce Springsteen and U2 raising millions of dollars for AIDS and world hunger. The Internet existed but none of us had e-mail, and the dot-com boom, with its gold-rush euphoria that money was everywhere to be made, was still a few years away. To be twenty at Harvard was to inhabit a world that was shiny and bright and moral—a world that might still be corrected. To be called an idealist was still high praise.

And yet, I had no idea how to imagine myself as a part of that world. Not even with Ray and Alexis's ambivalence, which seemed a sign of character. Before the accident, my default future was law school with a grudge, with a slim book of poetry hidden in my backpack. But now that track no longer seemed possible. Not because my grades had slipped, or because anything had changed outwardly, but because I knew it would be a lie.

So one blustery November afternoon, I went to see my advisor, Professor Coles. I'd liked him from the very first day in lecture, when he'd shuffled onstage in a gray moth-eaten wool sweater, his gray bushy hair looking moth eaten as well. Initially, I'd thought he was a homeless man who'd wandered into Sanders Theater in the midst of a delusion, his voice plaintive, filled with unease and conviction. But week after week, as though he'd rolled out of bed in the middle of the night and all 650 students were at his kitchen table, he talked about novels and about questions that gave him "pause." Intelligence, he seemed to be saying, was a fairly worthless faculty, even a shortcoming, unless it was employed in the service of leading a decent life.

His office was in Adams House, on the other side of the dining hall, in what had been FDR's dorm room. The bathroom still had a toilet with a pull chain and claw-foot tub, but Coles's updates were minor, as though he liked being partially an inhabitant of the past. Two small couches faced each other, with a Hopper print on one wall, a print of Robert Kennedy walking a dirt road in Wyoming on the other. No photographs of Coles with "big shots," as he called them, though he knew, I'd later learn, nearly every writer he mentioned in lecture, and he himself had been on the cover of *Time* magazine, his photo above the impossibly researched caption "America's top psychiatrist."

I settled into his white canvas couch, nervous to give up my role as star student, and more nervous to try on the role of patient. *Would he ask me to lie down? Should I tell him my dreams?* It wasn't appropriate, coming to him this way, but my pride didn't know what else to try. Besides, it seemed it would be fairly easy to steer the conversation away from my thesis on Ralph Ellison's *Invisible Man* and towards my own growing sense of invisibility, or heightened vision, or whatever it was. But, sinking into his couch, I didn't know how to start talking about the mornings on my bed, looking down onto Plympton Street and watching the rush up to class, how beneath my classmates moving like schools of fish, there seemed to be tides, sweeping them not just up to class but towards the future in particular directions, directions that didn't have to do with the moon or the tides but with societal forces that didn't make much sense. And I didn't know how to tell him that at night in the dining hall, the autumn air scraping at the high windows, I'd often find myself drifting on the background sound of conversation, as though the background had become part of the foreground, as though the far away had become near.

So I mentioned leaving the Office of Career Services Building that morning, where I'd been given biscotti and springwater, to find a homeless man on Mount Auburn Street wheeling a rickety shopping cart of aluminum cans.

Coles nodded. I'd intended to tell him about the blue binders, the job listings, how all the career paths seemed invalid because they had to blind you from what was outside them, like a horse's blinkers, so you kept on trotting forwards. The lines of my life had dissolved, and I wasn't about to sign up for new ones that were just as impermanent, just as likely to waver given a true test. But I was also afraid my new vision was just a vision, a mirage, something likely to fade over time.

But having mentioned the man with the shopping cart, I felt the emotion all over again, hot, embarrassing tears springing to my eyes.

"What is it?" Coles said.

I shook my head.

Outside his office door, students were on their way to class. Their footsteps clattered and faded down the tile corridor.

"What did you see?"

"His teeth," I said, my hand inadvertently rising to my own mouth. The man's face flashed in front of me. The horror of it. His mouth no longer a mouth. His teeth broken, bloodied. His pain broadcast for everyone to see, even if he didn't want to speak it.

Coles nodded.

"And just because I have a Harvard ID, I get free biscotti and springwater? I get binders full of jobs? I get the house in the suburbs?"

"What you're feeling," Coles said, "is a kind of moral disquiet."

It felt like a slap; he'd never talked to me with labels. "It's nice to give it a name, isn't it?" I said.

"And so to dismiss it?" he said testily.

I don't know what we said after that. I was still thinking about that man, about how it felt to be him, to walk the street with your mouth, your life, visibly broken. It disturbed me that

I knew nothing about him, couldn't imagine his life at all, and yet something about him felt personally familiar.

I backpedaled, made peace, couldn't risk opening up any further. Coles had always listened like no one I'd ever met, listened in a way that allowed me to hear the part of myself I was afraid of—the part that didn't fit with my family, the part that didn't really seem to fit anywhere, except in the realm of the writers we discussed. I couldn't afford to lose that, especially now, couldn't afford to discover there was a part of me he couldn't hear, or, worse, heard but disapproved of.

Towards the end of our talk, Coles asked if I'd noticed the binders for travel fellowships. There was one called the Rockefeller, he said, designed for students who had reached a crossroads in their lives.

"What senior hasn't reached a crossroads?" I said.

"You'd be a strong candidate," he said. "A very strong candidate, indeed."

The house was an enormous alarm far above me. My heart was pounding, something forcing me back up to the surface, pushing me up, up, up, past the bright coral and the strange fish of my dreams: something was happening up there, something important. Someone had died, someone had been hit by a car, someone was in the hospital.

I reached out for the phone beside the futon. The ringing stopped. The numbers glowed green in the dark room. "Hello!"

"Howie. It's Matt. You OK?"

Matt was my brother. He lived with his wife in Newton. I was in a house in Vermont.

"What is it?" I said. "What happened?"

"Nothing happened. Jesus. Don't tell me you were sleeping."

There was a permanent buzz on the line, like the droning

of a giant mosquito. "Just a second." I put down the phone, lit the candle on the low windowsill above the mattress. It was snowing outside, no moonlight, sweeps of snow brushed up against the screen. My heart was still going double time, still marching towards disaster. I didn't want Matt to hear it in my voice. "What time is it?"

"I got twenty minutes before *The West Wing* starts. Just thought I'd check in. You do know what *The West Wing* is."

I was trying to do the math. The sun probably set around four, I'd eaten a bowl of Ramen noodles for dinner, and then lay down by the fire. As usual, pictures had started to appear in my mind, and I'd fallen into a kind of visualization game. A month or so earlier, it had just started happening. And because it kept me company, I kept doing it. Some nights, I'd move through my morning walk to school as a boy—picturing it house by house, the tree roots buckling the sidewalk, past the Zandittens, the Longs, the white house with the black shutters whose family I didn't know, the Sugarmans, the Gorfinkles, the Donowitzes, the Cohens, then the left turn at the bottom of the hill, the stone retaining walls of the houses built on a slope, the yards waist-high, the plane trees with their peeling bark, loose sand still on the road after the winter snow had melted. Or I'd picture Bunk 7 from summer camp, going bed to bed, Josh Fields, Tom Carradine, Johnny Bent, Kevin Zolot, seeing how much I could recover of their blankets, their favorite t-shirts, their ways of talking, and then surprises would come: the job-wheel posted on the door, the Dopp kits arrayed on the bathroom shelves, the sharp smell of bleach, and those surprises would flare into something like short movies: the night of the sock war, a counselor slapping my hand as I reached for an ice cream sandwich, the first real conversation I had with Katherine Cohen outside Titus Hall, music from the Square Dance floating out over the soccer field. Lying on the wood floor, the firelight shimmering through the grate, I'd find myself laughing out loud or tears running from my eyes down into my ears. The stories would play on their own—some memories, some daydreams, as though I were watching my very own TV show. And then I'd come upstairs to bed.

I'd probably been asleep for a good two or three hours. "*The West Wing?*"

"Right," Matt said.

I saw the words in yellow and realized I was remembering the cover of *People* magazine from the checkout line at the C&C. "It's a TV show about the presidency," I said, my tone like a fortune teller reading a crystal ball. "With Martin Sheen. Very popular."

Matt's relief was audible. His brother's sense of reality was still intact. "So what's new?"

It seemed a strange question. "It's snowing. But that's not really new, I guess."

"Good, it's snowing. And?"

"Well, last night there was a full moon. The snow was blue and very bright. I could read by it." I decided not to mention the shadow of the branches on the snow, the way they looked like roots, as though the moonlight were letting me see underground. I decided not even to mention that normally I read by candlelight. I was doing a very good job sounding normal.

"Good. And?"

And what? It felt like a quiz. When I talked to Mom and Dad, which happened about once a month, Mom seemed relieved simply to know I was still breathing on the other end of the line, that I still remembered Star Market and the Sterns and Filene's Basement. When I talked to Dad, he asked questions with an implied correct answer: You feeling pretty good? (Yes.) And you're getting some exercise? (Yes.) And you're eating OK? (Yes.) Had he asked me about my bowel movements, I would have been happy to oblige. He was leading the witness, which was fine by me—we avoided the topic of my "living arrangement" by basically avoiding everything. But Matt was trickier. His ill-concealed frustration with my answers betrayed the questions he really wanted to ask. *What's wrong with you? Where's the guy I used to watch the Celtics with on the couch? What the fuck are you thinking?* But because they were questions he didn't know how to ask, and had answers I didn't know how to give, he treated me like a substitute for myself, a stand-in until his real brother returned.

"So, I read this book. Thought you might like it," he said.

This was a suspicious advance. "Really?"

"It's called *Into the Wild.* Ever hear of it?"

"I've seen *Into the Woods.*"

"It's a true story."

The phone mosquito hummed. My heart was hammering again. "What's it about?"

"A guy kind of like you. From the suburbs, athletic, went to Emory. Liked to read Tolstoy. But he hated society and went off to live in the Alaska woods."

"I don't hate society, Matt."

"No, of course you don't." I could see the look he was giving me across the miles—his mouth twisting, his eyes dark.

"So how does he get by?"

"He lives in an abandoned school bus."

"Did he have a woodstove inside?"

"I guess so. I don't know."

"And then what happens?"

The mosquito flew closer. A conversation was threatening, one Matt apparently had meant to imply but not begin. I could see him chewing at his lip, working the white scimitar of a scar he'd gotten when he'd crashed Mom's Volvo in high school. It was where his words went when he didn't know how to say them.

"The kid starves to death. That's what happens. He thinks he knows what plants he can eat, but he doesn't."

"Sounds inspirational."

"He poisoned himself."

"You mean on purpose?"

"Not on purpose. But he was ignorant. He didn't know what he was getting himself into."

"Did I mention I go to the market in town? That I eat frozen pizzas?"

"He went into the woods in April. He crossed this little stream to get to his school bus. But when he wanted to come back out, it was midsummer. The stream was a river. A raging river with all the snow that had melted."

"He couldn't ford it."

"No, he couldn't *ford* it. The way he'd gone in, it didn't lead back out."

I turned to look out the window. I'd been imagining a kid tromping around by an old school bus, dirty, happy, wild, but then he was standing on the bank, the stream gone muddy and violent. My stomach felt horrible. I had the feeling again of swimming up through my dreams too quickly. "There aren't any streams here," I said.

"Great. That's good to hear."

Part of me longed for him to say more, to explain more, but our man-to-man talk was clearly over. He'd already gone further than he wanted.

Years later, I'd learn that he'd been the one to push hardest while I was in the emergency room. He'd arrived in the rush-hour traffic, soon after my parents. Towards midnight, while I was in the bathroom throwing up from the pain, the ER doctors had held out one last chance: if a fragment of my optic nerve still held, it could possibly be bolstered by steroids. My vision might be saved. The doctors reminded Matt and my parents of the range of injuries to my eye, they rehearsed the risk of side effects. "Please," Matt had said. "Try anything." The doctors reminded him of the very slim odds, of the possible complications. But Matt had kept on pleading: "Please, try anything. He's my brother. Try anything."

As he switched the conversation now to running into someone from Roxbury Latin, my mind began to see the snowdrifts along the open field, the way they were piled so high. They'd never melt into a river. But my mind went on picturing them—like there might be some other version of that Alaskan river, some other blockade I couldn't yet imagine. Maybe the road in to the house wouldn't lead back out. Maybe it wouldn't be that simple.

Then I could hear a door closing, and Matt's wife, Jami, in the background. "Listen, our show is about to start," he said. "You take care, brother."

I hung up and the glow from the phone's numbers went away. The wind kicked up and snow brushed at the window screen. I didn't blow out the candle for some time.

Matt hit play on the VCR, and a little tuxedoed version of him introduced himself as the host of the show. "Today we're celebrating my little brother's graduation. But I wanted to give you all a glimpse of how he got here. Howie, *This Is Your Life*."

A murmur of laughter rippled the room. There were roughly thirty captive moviegoers: my parents, my grandparents, my closest friends and some of their parents—some sitting on the floor, on the couch, some standing in the back holding drinks or finishing their cake on little cardboard plates with balloons and mortarboards on them. *The party is here*, the plates and napkins read. I had been ushered up front, to the seat of honor.

The tuxedo vanished and Matt the reporter was standing on

the wood chips in front of Temple Beth Avodah nursery school, then in front of the white-washed bricks of the Baker School kindergarten, telling stories about me. His love was only going to make it worse. Now he was at Roxbury Latin. He shot the long, narrow corridors, the refectory with the Charles I coat of arms, the jaundiced gym. My college buddies continued the thread from the Adams House courtyard. One of my freshman-year roommates waxed nostalgic about girls asking for me before I'd even *arrived* on campus. And Andrew described my interrupting his last exam with forty minutes left on the clock, by telling the proctor his car was being towed from Mass. Ave. "By the way," he added, "I don't even have a car."

It was all true. The girls at the door freshman year. Springing my best friend from his last exam. I was the natural, the one who could breeze through anything. I felt the room looking back and forth between me and the TV, pleased with the resemblance. I heard my name again and again, but for the young man in the video, the accident hadn't happened. No one mentioned migraines or crashes. No one mentioned umbrellas or missed curbs or blind spots. It didn't matter that I hadn't confided in anyone about most of it. It didn't matter that my friends had no way of knowing how much my life had changed. What mattered was that my name kept going, and the picture kept forming, and it was just a memory, a picture from the past, which made me feel like a ghost from the future. No one alluded to the accident. I didn't want anyone to allude to it, but each successive story felt like another room added to a house that wasn't the house where I lived. Maybe it was a house I'd designed, maybe it was the one I wanted everyone to see, but standing outside it now with everyone, like there had just been a fire drill, when there had actually been a fire, felt terribly strange. It was as though the boy I'd hoped to see in the painting of the blue couch had finally arrived, but he wasn't the boy I'd been waiting for. The den was going farther away from me, as though my seat of honor was drifting out the window, as though I was looking in on a party for someone I didn't know. Maybe that was part of the physical strain, not just the love in the room but the awareness that everyone was seeing me off-center, horribly blurry—the strain of a blurred object not knowing how to get itself back into focus.

Mom broke into tears on the television. She was talking about my winning the Rockefeller, the fellowship that would send me to Italy for the next year. "You were just so confident. You just knew an interview was coming. You just knew." She was openly crying, waving the camera away. "Turn that thing off," she said. "Turn it off!" Dad, on the other chaise lounge on the back porch, held up my term bill for the camera. "Do you see what this is? Can you zoom on this? It says balance, zero. Congratulations! We made it. And congratulations on the Rockefeller! When you return from the year in Italy, maybe you'll apply for a Rhodes!"

No one in the room flinched. We had entered the realm of famous names now: Harvard, Rockefeller, Rhodes. And why not? We had all worked hard. We had all done our part. We had earned it. We, the Jews of Newburgh and Brookline, had arrived. Everyone was clapping, looking towards me. The video had ended.

I stood up, gave my brother a public hug. He was so large his embrace surrounded me like the shade of an enormous tree. I wanted to stay there as long as I could, to hide inside it, to emerge as someone other than the boy in the video. *Why had we all been unable to do this? Just to hold each other? To feel our pain against each other's arms?*

"Thank you," I said, stepping back.

"Congratulations," he said.

PART II

Learning to See

5

The red, white, and blue OPEN flag hung limp in the windless cold. The building looked less like a restaurant than a hunting camp—a brown cabin with two windows you couldn't see in, a screen door probably salvaged from somebody's back porch. The parking lot was empty. I considered walking back to the car, but the handwritten sign in the window advertised HOT PIZZA—steam waves rising from a sideways triangle—and I wasn't ready to return to the house. It was about a week before Christmas, and Nat had finally come to plow. I didn't know how long it'd be before I made it to town again, and I wanted to hear someone talk to me and to hear myself talk back. It was something to stock up on, like soup or frozen pizza, something I'd be able to replay in my mind at night by the fire, remembering how it felt. It would be a tether back to other people, something I could pull on when I felt myself floating too far away.

In the checkout line at the C&C, I'd been mesmerized by the cashier. Her eyes spiky with eyeliner, the crisp curls of her tightly permed hair, the swaying of her mustard yellow sleeves as her surprisingly well-manicured nails rang up the items, her eyes flicking between the price and the keys on the register, then down to the next item on the belt. We made no small talk. She said what the total came to and I paid. Only the conveyor belt was between us, and the wonder was different than the wonder of seeing a snail up close—it was more specific, more familiar. It made me aware of my hands. I was looking at one of my own kind. The oval shape of her face, the almond shape of her eyes.

The questions in my mind—*Where did she grow up? Who did she love?*—sent a current through me that didn't happen in the woods. They were questions I knew, questions a person could have asked me. Coming back into the parking lot, I'd felt a relief akin to the relief of coming out of a hospital. I could feel the diagnosis as I opened the car door, as I loaded my bag of groceries into the backseat: *still human.*

But I wanted to get a second opinion before returning to the house. I wanted to hear myself say something. To check on how the silence I'd been learning in the woods would turn into sound. More and more, as I snowshoed through the trees, as I sat by the woodstove at night, I felt something inside myself expanding, growing clear. That feeling I'd known as a boy at camp often spread through my chest, even beyond my chest, beyond my body, until there was no division between me and the land. But beyond the hills, where would that feeling lead? Could it fit into rooms and conversations? Not just into the stilted pauses on the phone with Matt but into something meaningful, something that had its own form? Could I carry it with other people—so that I'd stay grounded, in the most literal sense, so that I wouldn't lose myself again?

Inside the café, there was murky darkness. It took my eyes a moment to adjust. Two black tables sat beside the window, another two against the wall. There were no customers. I was just taking this in, relieved no one would look at me as I ate, when a woman shot out from the kitchen. "Well, hello. A good afternoon to you!" She unloaded a menu into my hand, her voice trailing behind her. "Table by the window?"

She moved with the electric jumpiness of a cartoon. "Right, let me tell you the specials of the house." She set a glass of water on the table, brushed the stringy gray hair from her shoulder with girlish flair. There was a hole in her wool sweater where the shoulder seam had pulled apart. Her voice was pitched for a party of eight. "We have Cornish pasties. A specialty. You're familiar with shepherd's pie?"

I unzipped my jacket.

"Right, then, a pasty is smaller. Filled with meat and onions and potatoes. All rolled in a nice pie and crimped on the side." Her eyes pulsed with over-determined focus, as though fighting against whatever hardship the rest of her had been through. Her accent—I wasn't imagining it—was British.

"You don't have pizza by the slice, do you?"

"We do have pizza! Bella," she called to the kitchen, her eyes still on me, "put the pizza oven on!"

"Yes, Mother!" a voice cried back.

"Now what kind would you like?"

I ordered a small cheese pizza and a Coke, which felt like a tremendous indulgence. It would come to $6.25, including tax.

"Very good," the woman said. "Bella," she called. "Do come out and say hello!" It was as though I had come calling and presented my card. The kitchen door swung open and a very tall girl with sparkling silver hair came out.

"Do take that off."

The girl reached up to her head. "I forgot," she said. She pulled the wig from her head, revealing a lush tangle of blonde hair. It was clear she had preferred the wig.

"This is Bella, my daughter," the woman said.

I said hello.

The girl, who was probably six feet tall and no more than seventeen years old, curtsied theatrically, flashing a fake smile at her mother. Her body was ungainly, unformed, it seemed, by movies, by magazines, by any sense of the shape she was supposed to fit into, her hips up to her ears. But her face had the startling beauty of a Renaissance madonna.

"And I'm Linda," the woman said, extending her hand. Her grip was shockingly strong. "Your pizza shouldn't be long."

The room settled back into subterranean murk. I took off my jacket. I was relieved by the proprietress and her daughter—they seemed almost as peripheral to the town as I was. No gossipy waitress interviewing me about my doings in these parts. No short-order cook giving me the stink eye through his window. This café was just what I needed. To see people without the threat of being seen. To be able to sit somewhere public without having to situate myself in any public way. It was like a scrimmage, a dry run. Being with people without being with too many people.

Besides, it was pleasant to be sitting somewhere that wasn't the house—to be out on the town. And it was doubly pleasant to be somewhere communal that was quiet. In the C&C, I struggled not to be overwhelmed by the top 40 radio station playing from the market's overhead speakers. At the house there was no reason to dim my hearing. There was no sound that wasn't useful. I wanted to hear the fire—to know from the wind-rush and the popping if it was burning too hot—and to hear the birds—for their song and their company—and to hear anything, even if it was just a squirrel, that was approaching in the woods. My hearing had never been more acute or more necessary. But at the entrance to the C&C, when Elton John surrounded me between the sets of automatic doors, I felt as though a carnival ride were whisking me off the ground. I clutched the chilled handle of the shopping cart, did my best to keep a measured pace into the frozen foods, but inside me a roller coaster filled with teenagers sped and plunged, their hair flying straight up in the wind. *LA, la, la, la, la, LA!* "Crocodile Rock" bounced beneath the Elio's pizza boxes, making the freckled girl on the pink package of ice cream cones smile, loosening up the Jolly Green Giant in his green singlet of leaves. It bounced under the very tile of the aisles, and I didn't understand how the slowly trolling matrons in housecoats weren't all feeling it too. I avoided their eyes, tried to behave as though I was in a library, but as the song ended, and the prospect of quiet marketing returned, there was Whitney Houston, desperate to dance with somebody—*with SomeBody WHO, SomeBody WHO*—and the wild-eyed cartoon rabbits and neon-colored birds on the cereal boxes looked as though they wanted to jump down from their cardboard warrens and nests and twirl with her down the aisle. The music was sugar in my veins. I caught myself tapping my thumbs on the shopping cart, smiling like a madman. Plus, there were the jingles and commercials sweeping off the boxes and jars as I walked past—*Choosey Moms Choose Jif, Have a Coke and a Smile, Help Yourself to Stouffer's Pizza.* Each product seemed designed for customers who couldn't see very well, the words and colors like the orange semaphores used to guide a plane. It all fizzed together to make me feel like I was traveling through a parallel land, something like Oz, only more familiar because it was the America I'd grown up with. Swiss Miss, Aunt Jemima, Count Chocula, the Sun Maid! They were all garishly reassuring—welcoming me back to their version of reality, which I was still invited to as long as I had a bit of cash. When I made it back to the house, a party would still be buzzing inside me. As I unpacked the groceries, Elton John and Whitney Houston would come tumbling back out, as though from a music box, down to which lyrics had carried me through which aisles. The Stouffer's pizza was still broadcasting: *Oh lawdy mama, those Friday nights, when Suzie wore her dresses tight.* The box of Life cereal: with *somebody WHO, somebody WHO.* The food somehow contained the songs, which themselves contained a map of my progress through the store. My senses were so open, my attention so available, that I'd absorbed it all without trying. Maybe my brain was still adapting, joining my vision and hearing together, somehow making everything easier to remember. Or maybe I was just starved for stimulation. Or maybe some primal instinct for map making, for orientation, had returned.

Anyway, it was pleasant now just to sit in the restaurant's quiet. After some harried discussion from the kitchen I couldn't quite decipher, the tall girl came back with my glass of Coke. She set it down on the table. She hovered. To be so close to another person without words felt dangerous.

"You go to the regional high school?" I said.

"Mom homeschools me. *Homeschools*, that's a verb. We run the gamut. Even biology, which I loathe, but I suppose cells are people too. Or something like that. Our curriculum is really quite comprehensive."

"It sounds it."

"Yesterday, for instance, I was reading about zygotes. Do you know about zygotes? Do people walk down the street with thoughts of zygotes running through their heads? I certainly hope not. But I wonder. What if I'm the only one walking down the street with thoughts of zygotes? You know? Wouldn't that be peculiar?"

I considered. "Or with thoughts about those thoughts."

Her eyes brightened. "Yes, exactly! Which probably makes me more peculiar still!"

"Or maybe just the opposite."

"Maybe. Would you like to see me juggle? I've been practicing."

She ran off to the kitchen. I took a long sip from my Coke. It was strangely exhilarating to be talking with another human being—and at such speed. I was doing well! It felt like playing a sport—the movement, the unpredictability. The way each response depended on the last, the way you carried each other forward, the way the words had a direction but could swoop and shift, like birds playing in the air. I'd forgotten the thrill. Did people really do this all the time—minute after minute, hour after hour?

I told myself to be careful. She was so young. Which was reason enough. Besides, I knew from my years on the road my propensity for shifting my attention to a woman, letting my reflection in her eyes stand in for what I was searching for, tending to her wounds so I could run from my own. It was a bad song on repeat after my return from Italy. It happened in New Mexico with Ani, then in Arizona with Jillian, then in Montana with Melissa. Thinking myself a kind, genuinely interested fellow, I heard their stories and then had their ankles around my ears. And then I left. With an earnest good-bye, with an explanation about needing to go on searching, but what did it matter? Their letters, which I'd receive months later back in Boston, made a collection. *The walk along the river . . . the hike through the canyon . . . the rain . . . the sun. . . . why are you so guarded ? . . . you give with one hand, take away with the other . . . no, I understand perfectly what you were saying, what you were saying is that you're an asshole.* Which is part of why I'd come to Vermont and moved into solitude, so I couldn't hurt or hide in anyone, so I couldn't go on stalling with some disposable version of myself. Whatever I was going to find, however I was going to get my bearings, I didn't want it to be in relation to anything that wasn't permanent—I didn't want it to be *relative*. I needed to find something that couldn't be taken away and that I couldn't leave.

She was wearing her silver wig. All hips and elbows and overeagerness. It almost made me feel safe—she was so young. "I'll just start with three, but I can work my way up to five." The beanbags started flying.

"Bella!"

"I must away," she said, setting the beanbags on the table as though I might want to try them for myself. They were made of blue denim and patches from a red bandanna. I didn't touch them. I knew from my nights by the woodstove how dangerous even the most basic fantasies could be. The space inside me was too large, the stage in my mind too vacant. The images would get away from me and start following their own currents, just like dreams.

The mother burst through the swinging door. I realized I'd been holding one of the beanbags and hurriedly put it back on the table. She scooped them up, deposited them in her apron, and set down the pizza. The steam rose luxuriously off the cheese.

"Buon appetito!" she said.

A negative space of fireworks was beginning in my mouth.

"I hope she didn't juggle your ear off."

"Not at all."

"She's really a very intelligent girl. She just lacks company." She rested her hand on the back of the chair opposite me.

"Understandable."

"Right, well."

She wasn't returning to the kitchen. She was contemplating the chair. To my surprise, I kind of wanted her to sit—but I didn't want to want her to sit, didn't want to trade stories of how we came to be in this town, didn't want to reassure her about her daughter and begin some sideways seduction, didn't want to get involved.

"The pizza's very good."

"Splendid, thank you!" She clapped her hands together. "Well, we certainly hope you'll come back and see us again soon. You live here in Barton?"

"Close by."

She waited, but I didn't elaborate. "Excellent. I'll leave you to your food."

I was able to manage only two small slices, half the Coke. I was surprised I couldn't eat more. My stomach had probably shrunk. As I zipped up my coat to leave, the two of them hovered by the kitchen door. "Ciao, signore," Bella said.

"Ciao, tutti."

"But you speak Italian?" the mother said.

I was sorry for it. "Yes."

"Ah! La prossima volta, parliamo italiano!"

Now they both looked at me far too openly, mother and daughter, their faces a harmony of hungers. I looked down at my box of leftovers. I was ashamed of how much their loneliness pulled on me, how ready they would be to tell their stories, and how ready I would be to listen, and to listen, and to listen.

My fellowship in Italy had only two stipulations: not to enroll in any formal plan of study and not to marry. The Rockefeller was designed for "a journey of adventure and discovery at a vulnerable and pivotal time in one's life," and apparently marrying or studying would interfere. Tie me to the mast—I was pretty sure I could handle it. I rented a room in a house in the hills outside Bologna. My window looked out on a vineyard, which sloped down towards a two-lane road, and across the road the hills rose in a patchwork of fields—some smooth and green, some striped with the slender rows of grapevines, some just clumped earth from which dust would rise up in the wind. Horses, the size of my thumbnail from the window above my desk, would appear in the afternoon. Long heads lowered to the land, something strangely elemental and hieroglyphic about their four legs walking. At the base of the hills, the road billowed in slow curves, following the narrow stream that ran through the valley.

I sat at my makeshift desk—an old door, with a missing doorknob, over two sawhorses—considering for the first time what I might have to say and how I might say it. I had begun reading fiercely, unabashedly, trying to figure out how I might write a novel. There was no one to hide my reading habit from anymore, no one I saw on a daily basis, no one for whom I was supposed to play a role. My landlord didn't care what I did in my room as long as I was quiet and paid my rent. She'd leave a pot of rabbit stew for me on the stove; she'd make toast every morning promptly at eight, whether I wanted to eat it or not. She was in her midforties, attractive, utterly uninterested in discussion. Cooking, she said, was part of the rent—but not company. I rarely saw her. Occasionally, I'd notice I'd lost a whole day to a book; even when I stepped outside for a walk, I was still having conversations with the characters in my mind. It was the first period in my life when my thoughts had full license to expand. Nothing going on inside me had to be tamed—I didn't see people, didn't have to organize myself into a person for anyone's eyes. The books piled up haphazardly on my nightstand. *Rabbit Run*, *Van Gogh's Letters to Theo*, *Il Cavaliere Inesistente*, *The Collected Chekhov*, *A Farewell to Arms*—anything I could find on my landlady's bookshelf in English or Italian. I began recording passages in the journal Mom and Dad had bought me for the trip. Such sweet heresy! It had an old-fashioned sun on the cover, a face with rays shooting out in all directions, but it looked to me like a boy with his face pressed to the porthole of a ship. My hope was that the quotations accumulating on the pages behind his eyes would eventually give way to the words behind my own. I wasn't dreaming of best sellers. But I did imagine finding the shape of the world again beneath my pen; I did imagine being able to tell fellow readers how I saw. Which meant, really, I was imagining being less alone.

Day after day, I'd stare out at the neat rows of grapevines, then at my own tangle of words, then back at the grapevines. The room really did look like the room of a writer. The notes by the computer, the stack of books by the bed. I'd sold the Rockefeller committee on having a *unique perspective*, on seeing *behind the façade of daily life*. But to have a perspective you needed to be seeing from somewhere, to be located, and I didn't feel located at all. I didn't belong to any place. I'd go for long walks. I'd get up to use the bathroom when I didn't have to. Maybe if I read just one more novel, looked up a few more words in the enormous English dictionary in the hall. I was a twenty-two-year-old who needed to be starting in the mailroom, and I'd found myself in the corner office, painfully aware I didn't deserve to be there.

Ilaria, my landlord, hardly blinked when I told her I was moving down into Bologna. Devoting all my energies to being less alone had, in fact, only made me lonelier—and I needed to spend more time with people. I didn't really need to explain; loneliness was something she could understand. Her husband, a dentist, was having an affair with a university student and had moved out months before my arrival. He had isolated her, she said, here in the hills. *Isolata*—the word from *isola*, meaning island. She had a mole just to the side of her mouth, her dark eyes somewhere between alluring and haggard. Every afternoon her tiny red Alfa Romeo would escape down the dusty hillside between the rows of grapes, a cloud of dust trailing behind it. What she did on her outings in Bologna I never knew: maybe she had a lover, maybe she shoplifted the lipsticks she expertly applied while she drove, maybe she watched movies, one after the next, sitting in the dark. We were in her car, driving to the market in town, when I told her. It was January, the air had grown chill. She wore a black turtleneck sweater and sat very straight. I knew she needed the rent money, but she said nothing. Something about her calmness suddenly made me think she did spy on her husband, that she followed him beneath porticoes, waited for him outside apartments. At the very least, it was clear that whatever bitterness brought the bright edge to her eyes, she had once been very much in love.

"Go the city," she said. "I understand."

"You do?"

"You want love," she said. "You want to know your heart. You can only find this with another person, no?"

Not far past the buried stone wall, by the intertwined birches that arched over the trail, I stopped to listen. Two chickadees were singing back and forth, a two-note song, slow and plaintive: *Fee-bee. Fee-bee.* In between the calls, there was just silence, the sound of my own breathing. The calls seemed to hang the woods like an enormous tapestry, to stretch the air and the trees to their proper proportions. But I couldn't see the birds. At each note, my eyes climbed branch after branch, scurrying higher up, farther back, but there was only the intricate white latticework of the branches. The song went again. *Fee-bee. Fee-bee.* But I saw nothing.

They had been my best neighbors all fall, a rare flash of movement among the leaves, little black and white sparks more curious than the squirrels. On the dirt road, a flying fist would follow me, its jumpy flight pattern so close I could hear the thrum of its wings—the rise, after every floating dip, fired by a wing burst, a tiny fusillade of flight. When I stopped, a chickadee would suddenly alight on a nearby branch and wait, its small round black head, with the racy white bank-robber's mask, adjusting left, adjusting right, a charade of curiosity. *Oh, really? Really?* it seemed to say. The more I encountered them on my walks, the easier it was to understand Native American legends of *coyote* or *fox*—each black-capped chickadee a particular companion but also becoming a part of the idea of *chickadee*, some playful and intrepid winter spirit of the woods. I couldn't help liking them. To walk the road, even when no chickadee appeared, was to feel its company, to remember the small, inquisitive face from the day before. It was my court jester, my Northeast Kingdom little fool. But now, for whatever reason, the chickadee was done showing itself. The white mask had slid off its face, expanded, and become the entire snowy woods.

I jammed my poles in the snow. Damn little birds. My encounter at the café was still humming inside me, and I wondered if that's why I couldn't see. The girl juggling in her silver wig, the mother's hand on the back of the chair, the way they looked at me as I left. It was one thing at the C&C to stand close to the cashier—usually it took an afternoon to settle back into the visual quiet of the woods, to stop having flashes of spiky eyelashes and the colorful array of foods—but something deeper had been stirred up this time, a readiness I'd forgotten about, and it seemed a grave weakness, something that could lead to a derailment of why I'd come to the woods. I felt like the second monk in the famous story about the woman crossing the muddy road. The first monk picks her up and carries her across the mud, so her kimono won't get stained, but the second monk becomes greatly agitated as the two monks continue on their way, "Why did you do that? You have betrayed our oath!" The first replies, "I put her down on the far side of the road, but you are still carrying her." It's not that I thought of myself as a monk, but if I was going to be *like* one of the monks in the story, I at least wanted to be the virtuous one—the one pure of mind rather than pure of deed, the one who follows the spirit of the law rather than the letter. And the spirit of my own law meant that I wasn't supposed to think about anyone in town, wasn't supposed to think about any kind of relationship. It would be an easy way out, a shortcut to identity, a way of making myself feel good that I wasn't ready for and didn't deserve. I worried I was still carrying the mother and daughter with me. And the woods seemed to agree. They weren't taking me back so quickly.

I looked down at my snowshoes, rested my neck and shook my head, trying to clear the inside of my eyes. By the time I looked up again, my eyes were soft. Just the tangle of the high branches, the blue palm of the sky. I wanted to calm myself, to let my vision go wide, to feel myself not trapped inside branch after branch, to see without the possibility of any labyrinth. And then there was a streak. A gray blur lifting from one tree to another. My eyes didn't chase. The blur went again, a bit to my left. And there, hunched in a ball against the wind, feathers slightly ruffled, adjusting itself on a snowy twig, was a bird. Tiny black head cocking left, cocking right. My heart rushed. It wasn't so high up after all. My long lost friend! I wanted to raise my arms in greeting! And, with another blur, there was the other one, just a few trees away. I had slipped behind the mask—here we all were together!

Eventually, as I resumed snowshoeing up the hill, my error dazzled me. Instead of just looking for a change in the air, I'd been hunting for an individual chickadee—a little tuft of gray and white and black in the snowy trees—which meant training my eyes only to see one thing and effectively blinding myself to everything else. But relaxing my eyes, and opening my gaze to movement, was to allow myself to see the smallest changes, to see, in a way, what the forest saw: the space between the trees, the lines of the branches, and any movement that might happen there. Maybe this was the way to see, to let my eyes be like ears, simply open to space and whatever might enter it: no limit on depth, no limit on possibilities. I pushed up to the top of the rise and looked out over the vista. The sky was perfectly clear—pale blue above the far white mountains and darkening blue up the vault.

As I stood still, breath smoking in the cold, I had the feeling that the mountains were a true mirror, because they didn't *try* to see, didn't get lost in the vast surface of details. They excluded nothing. There was no part of me they didn't accept. And the reflection they offered would never shatter: no accident or heartbreak could take it away. It was essential, not relative. They just needed more time to give me a reflection that was a little more solid—something I could take back to the daily world.

"Fuck, come on, man. Real life. Real girls." Juan Ignacio's voice could have been a neon sign with a woman's legs kick-kicking from a martini glass. I tried to think of *A Moveable Feast,* of the literary buddy stories I'd been lapping up in my room in the hills outside Bologna. The women and the cafés. The conversations and the exploits. Albeit expressed a bit more gracefully, this was why I'd moved down into the city. But it was late March now, and all I'd done since moving in two months earlier was to read, to write, and to wander the city on my own.

"Just give me a minute," I said.

After checking my hair in the bathroom mirror and finding it a lost cause, I followed Juan Ignacio's long back up the drafty stairwell. Music throbbed from the front room, and through the doorway there were the shapes of people dancing. The apartment was laid out just like ours—the same long, narrow corridor with the same windows on the courtyard. Young Italian families occupied the lower floors of the building, their laundry lines suspended over the courtyard, and international twenty-somethings, mostly students in the Johns Hopkins graduate program for international relations, lived upstairs. I followed Juan Ignacio through a palisade of faces and hands, a receiving line minus the wedding, with lots of German and cigarette smoke. Faces kept peering at me, dazzling and bright, and I couldn't tell if it was with interest or concern. A lit cigarette brushed too close to my hand. Lipstick bunched on a woman's lips. Maybe I really had spent too much time alone in the hills. After securing two cups of wine in the kitchen, Juan Ignacio led me back into the room with the dancing. I was just beginning to consider how long it would be before I left when I noticed a woman. She was talking with two well-dressed men, her hips still in rhythm but the music nothing that was carrying her. One man, with thin blond hair to his shoulders, was smiling, as though the conversation and the music were all one thing. The other man, who was handsome, looked a bit uneasy and was hardly dancing at all. The woman wore a white blouse open at the collar. Her neck was long, her hair up on her head. She seemed to be enjoying herself but ready at any moment to step through a door and find herself somewhere else, someplace better.

The dance music changed to a Donna Summer remix, and I felt an odd little surge of confidence. Not in America, it was easy to feel patriotic, to muster a healthy American disdain for Germans dancing to disco. Besides, I'd always loved parties in college—the dancing, the alcohol, the feeling of something hidden moving below the floor, something rising and starting to emerge. Juan Ignacio joined a group of friends and I didn't follow. The faces and bodies felt too close, and I wanted the wall behind me to recede, so there'd be more space between me and the dancers. I could see the woman in the white blouse so clearly. The play of her hips beneath her long skirt, the expression on her face. I tried to look away, but I was pretty sure she wanted to say something to me. The two men kept dancing beside her. Her mouth, which was strong, her teeth slightly too large, gave the impression that she was about to speak. She recognized me, I was almost sure, and she was on the verge of mouthing something—to ask where we'd met, or if I wanted to dance.

The song changed again. There was no way I wouldn't have remembered her. My mind tore through my past—through bus stations and piazzas and museums, through lecture halls and airports and summer camp, even through New York City, where

I'd once tried to memorize the faces of girls at Grand Central, wondering who they were, where they came from, suddenly dizzyingly aware of the number of girls I would glimpse once and probably never see again, suddenly dizzyingly aware, beneath that enormous ceiling adorned with the constellations, of the role chance could play in a life. But the dancing woman was nowhere. Not rising out of any summer stream, not stepping onto any train, not walking beside me down any street.

As I looked at her again, a sudden longing overwhelmed me. I wanted my past to be different—for my life to be different, so that it might have included her.

"Are you Italian?"

The song had ended, I'd gone to the window for air, and she was standing beside me. I had the momentary feeling that I'd willed her there. "American."

Something in her eyes stalled.

"Is it so bad?"

"*Naya*," she said. "My name is Milena."

"Naya?"

"Naya. It means no and yes. But at the same time." She smiled lightly, a smile at herself. "This is very Viennese."

The man with the long blond hair was clearly watching us. "Would you like to get a drink?"

"We go to the roof."

I followed her to the kitchen for more wine, fearing a series of delays and introductions, but she moved purposefully through the crowd. The stairwell rose one more floor, the air immediately looser, the music blurring behind us. We passed through a door that said only *attenzione*.

A crescent moon hung in the sky. I'd expected the roof to be a kind of party satellite, but maybe the others didn't know about it. We were alone. The March air bit with a pleasant sharpness. We could see the terra-cotta rooftops, the Due Torri lit from below, and Piazza Maggiore glowing like the courtyard of a medieval palace. She rested her wine on the parapet.

"Would you say the moon tonight is naya?" You could see the crescent, but you could also see the part of it that was dark. Apparently, the guard who checked the normalcy papers of my comments had nodded off in his booth.

She tilted her head to the side, dim light catching her neck. "But naya does not usually mean this." She almost smiled. "So you are the American writer, no?"

I did my best to sound modest and impressive.

"Do you know Musil?" she said.

"No."

"Goethe?"

"Not personally."

She made a face. I was becoming more American by the second. "Herman Hesse?" she said, clearly throwing me a bone.

"Hesse! I read *Siddhartha* when I was sixteen. At this real estate office where my father found me a job. I read and forgot to answer the phone."

"Exactly. You know *Narcissus and Goldmund*?"

I wasn't about to lose the little ground I'd gained. "Tell me about it."

"Now, this is very teenager experience, but when I am fourteen, I read this book. It is the story of two young men who meet in a monastery school. One is quiet and studies hard and reads Greek and Latin and so. The other is beautiful and likes to adventure and to live. I read it in summer, at my grandmother's house in the Steiermark. For days I do not go with the others to swim in the lake. I do not go to the meals. I sit in the garden and read and wonder which character I am more similar to. But I want to be both. Is this not strange? Even then I know the book is obvious. It is supposed to be obvious. You are supposed to find a compromise between them—to live part adventure, part study.

But it is not obvious to me. I want to be both of them, completely. I sit in the garden with my too-big sunhat, and I want to go everywhere and to read everything. But when my friend Sophie asks me to walk in the mountains or to swim, I don't want to go. Nothing is fast enough. Nothing outside is big enough for what I feel inside. You must know this feeling, no?"

I was stunned. The chill night air had slipped inside my shirt, but I tried to hide it. I had the sense this woman knew more about me than I knew about myself. "I guess it's a feeling of not knowing where to start."

She squeezed my arm. "Ya, exactly," she said. Her touch rattled through my body.

The music from the party downstairs had drifted far away. We went on talking. It was as though there was no possibility of misunderstanding, because the words meant so little, were just approximate shapes for what we felt, and what we felt had somehow arrived before us—more like a frequency we were hearing, or a certain hue that was part of the air.

The conversation lasted maybe seven minutes. When we were both starting to shiver, we went back downstairs, but I didn't return to the party. I didn't want to lose the feeling. She needed to return to her friends, and I didn't want to chance feeling jealous or out of place. I continued downstairs to my room, took a long hot shower, then lay on top of the blanket. The music was still throbbing above me, drifting down into the courtyard. I remembered the way she had looked at me while she was dancing, like she recognized me. She hadn't been mistaking me for someone else.

6

I was nervous to be bringing them to the house. Linda had said they needed a Christmas tree. They didn't have a car, they couldn't afford a delivery—they possibly were trying to hire a ride up to Newport. But I knew they couldn't afford it. The café was just as bereft of customers the second time I went. Bella's sweatshirt had the same penguins pulling the same polar bear on the same sled; Linda's gray sweater was still unmended. Linda had sounded defeated, ready to concede, a Christmas tree a convention she and her unconventional daughter could do without. They had a parakeet, Mr. Kipling, and Mr. Kipling and a few bags of microwave popcorn were all the cheer they needed. It wasn't so much her loneliness as her resignation to her loneliness that got me. Maybe it struck a chord with some fear I had about myself—some future I didn't want to admit as a possibility. Anyway, I may have been a Jew and a hermit, but I wasn't the Grinch, was I? Pine saplings dotted the top of the incline where I left my car; an axe and a rusted hacksaw waited in the mudroom. And these two displaced British women weren't expecting anything, which made it possible to offer. It would just be a tiny Christmas miracle, with no expectation of anything to follow. The whole expedition—picking them up, felling the tree, driving them home—would cost me nothing. At least that's what I'd told myself.

It was a bright, windy late afternoon, and they were waiting outside the café, playing some kind of hand-clapping game in the cold. Linda wore a thin scarf tied roguishly around her neck—part high fashion, part Huckleberry Finn. Bella, in her enormous Michelin Man coat, looked ready for Siberia. They were giddy. From their faces, you might have thought suitcases were waiting at their feet and we were setting out to drive cross-country, wild adventures ahead.

"You're sure. You're absolutely sure," Linda said, the car door open, the cold whipping in.

"Yes."

"There must be quite a lot of trees, of course."

"Mother, just get in."

Bella was already in the backseat. Linda closed her door, smiled at me—gratitude flavored with conspiracy. I wondered how long they'd been out in the cold.

"Nice car. Does your radio work?" Bella said.

"Bella!" Linda said.

I flipped it on—there was static, the sound of the empty street, of long skies and coming snow. No one was out in town, everyone probably already inside with their families, baking cakes, wrapping presents, touching up the ornaments on their trees. The truth was, I didn't really know what most people did on Christmas, only that it was usually nice to be with my own family not doing whatever those things were. We didn't have any Jewish Christmas rituals—no Chinese food, no going to the movies. We were more or less left out of America for the day, but we were left out together.

Only two stations surfaced through the static in English, and we drove through the pre-holiday quiet to commercials for snowmobiles and truck dealerships. I feared "White Christmas" coming on—this non-Grinch thing could only go so far—but as we turned onto Roaring Brook Road, a familiar chord hit.

DOES he love me, I want to know, HOW can I TELL if he LOVES me so?

Bella launched into full lip sync in the backseat, shaking her long blonde hair back and forth, and Linda executed a half turn, first just to smile, then big-eyeing it with her. As we passed the abandoned county fairground—the hand-painted sign for Aug. 23 still posted above the snow—I couldn't help feeling it too: the easy champagne of the music, the lift of being in the car and going somewhere, of not being alone, of having a kind of mission. We were going to chop down a tree. We were a *group* now, my little Honda a quietly rollicking Merry Band of Misfits.

"How far is your house?"

"About ten more miles."

"Very well," Linda said, adjusting her scarf. I wasn't sure if she wanted the trip to be longer or shorter.

As we turned onto the dirt road, crossed the snow mud-stained with tractor tracks, and continued up into the woods, the intoxication subsided. The station was going scratchy. I switched the radio off. We followed past the trailers, into the thicker snow of the unmaintained lane, and the silence of the trees surrounded us. I had the feeling that I was taking them inside my mind. I pictured them as though inside a crystal ball, caped wayfarers exploring some unmapped region, the forking paths into the woods really just various substructures of my consciousness. The thought was horrifying—far too interior. I didn't want anyone that close.

Linda pulled at her cuticles. Bella hummed to herself. I was a man they didn't know, taking them to a cabin in the woods. A cabin with an axe and a hacksaw. It occurred to me I should say something. The silence in the car was a silence for one, un-comfortable with three, and I knew I should be putting them at ease. But I couldn't play tour guide. I couldn't translate. To talk about the land would have felt like I was talking about myself. Just having them with me, where I had only been alone, was already a kind of conversation, an intimacy I didn't know how to understand.

"It's so far away," Bella said. The snowy road rolled silently beneath us.

"Patience," Linda said.

We passed the open field, pushed through the drifts, and I parked in the small plowed-out space, the lone human accommodation, at the top of the grade. As we got out of the car, I didn't say anything. I wanted the place to speak for itself, like an abandoned cathedral, its hush still in the air. When I returned from town, my only customary routine was to piss in the snow— less to mark the territory than to feel myself back in the woods, back in the wild. I didn't suggest it now. But I was conscious of moving more slowly than I had in town, of feeling oddly proud of the apple trees outlined and shimmering with snow, of the majestic display of the pines.

They followed me down towards the house. A skein of smoke was still rising from the chimney.

"It's quite big, isn't it?" Linda said. Snow glinted off the sloping roof of the garage. A jagged palisade of icicles hung from the beaten deck outside my room.

"It looks enchanted," Bella said.

The rustling of our jackets and our boots squeaking against the snow were oddly loud, like we were an invading battalion. I didn't want to make them wait in the cold, but I didn't want them inside the house.

"I'll just need to get the axe and saw."

We passed through the store of firewood, the muted light, the cold cottony smell of the wood. They made no sign of dropping behind. They expected to come in. To leave them in the garage would have been cruel.

"We'll just go into the mudroom," I said.

But as we stepped inside, the soiled musk of dead mouse unmistakable in the walls, the telephone began to ring. It hadn't rung in weeks. "Excuse me," I said, trying to sound routine. I opened the door to the house, tracked snow past the woodstove, picked up the phone. "Hello."

"You were out walking?"

The voice sounded parched and small. "Yes. How are you, Lev?"

"And you have shoveled the roof? And cleaned the chimney?"

"Yes," I said, answering the first question, not the second. "How are you?"

"Not so great. I make this brief—the long-distance rates, you don't believe." I could see him running his hand through his thinning red hair, the wind hot on the windowpane of some unkempt apartment.

"What is it?"

"Grossman left. He is also in the department. Was. Was in the department. So we have few options for next year. I must stay in Tel Aviv. It is not so bad here. But the house. I dream last night of coming back to animals. You know this Bear Jamboree?"

I had to think. "At Disney World?"

"Yes, it is horribly fake. Horribly American, if you excuse me. But I dream of coming back and there is the bear jamboree. Inside my house. The bears playing instruments. You can stay? Same agreement. No rent. Only wood and electricity. This is acceptable?"

Bella and Linda were bickering in the mudroom like they were back in the kitchen at the café. I carried the phone away from the woodstove, closer to the window. "I'll have to think about it, Lev."

"The department meeting is soon. They need an answer."

I tried to imagine another winter. Outside, a fringe of birch bark tattered in the wind. The trees were so still. All I could see was quiet. But it came more easily than imagining the alternative. The loneliness would be bad, but anything else would be worse. Back in Boston, I couldn't see myself, couldn't see anything. The curtain of my mind wouldn't open.

"I'll think about it."

"Good! Very good! Excellent! I go now. We talk in another week. Good-bye!"

Out the long windows to the woods, the land around the house felt vast, suddenly expanded. I could hear Bella and Linda in the mudroom, but their voices had gone farther away. This was becoming my life. The stillness of the days. The long quiet of the nights. The fire in the woodstove. This was becoming who I was. And the only thing that disturbed me was how natural it felt: the voice that should have been raging against staying—*What are you thinking? Remember the boy in the bus!*—had drifted farther away, too.

I returned to the mudroom, gathered the axe and the hacksaw, and we headed outside into the cold. I was relieved to have Bella and Linda with me, relieved to see the eagerness, however sobered, still in their faces. Maybe I could learn to bring them into my life here—maybe I could move one step in from the periphery of the periphery. Maybe I'd even cook them dinner one night. I had a fleeting image of myself running a Christmas tree farm—an article in the *Newport Chronicle* about the young Jew who sells trees.

"Look, can you imagine?" Bella said, pointing towards the tallest spruce. "You'd need scaffolding!"

"And a house without a roof," Linda said.

I could feel the weight of the axe on my shoulder. It was heavier than I'd expected. The hacksaw was badly rusted, orange corroding the sharp teeth, but the axe might do the trick. "You said a sapling, right?"

"Of course. Nothing much taller than Bella."

"Do you think it will still smell like the woods?" Bella said.

Linda looked at me hopefully.

"It should," I said, unsure if I was playing expert or father, but not too keen on either role.

They chose a pine sapling not far from the apple trees. It wasn't very robust, some threadbare gaps towards the top, but it would do. The axe was terribly dull. I got through the bark, the pulp white as an exposed shin, but my hands were turning raw.

"Can I have a go?" Bella asked. "Just a swing or two?"

I looked at Linda. Her face was open—she was far too ready to defer to my judgment. This short trip, this standing around in the cold, was probably the closest she'd come to a vacation in months. Her trust made me uneasy, but I handed Bella the axe.

She swung, missed, swung again. The thin top branches shivered with the blow. She'd probably never taken a gym class, never played a sport, and her body was wild with untrained energy. Her cheeks flushed red, her hair whipped around her face. The axe kept corkscrewing her around, until it looked like she might hit her own leg.

Feeling disturbingly paternal, I told them the axe was too dull, which it likely was, and took up the hacksaw and cut through the slender trunk. We drove back to town with the windows open, taking the turns very slowly, each of us with one arm on a branch, the tree shifting side to side on the roof. Linda directed me. They lived about a quarter-mile behind the café, on a street with very modest houses, narrow driveways between them. A few wreaths on the doors, no Christmas light displays, no plastic reindeer out front.

"This has been very kind of you," Linda said, her hands already in the tree's branches. "You must need to get going."

"It's no problem."

"We can manage," she said glancing behind her towards the house. "Thank you very much."

"Mom, let him help," Bella said.

Linda wouldn't look at me.

"Let me help."

"Oh, very well then, but keep your eyes closed. I haven't tidied. Really, you must understand."

We small-stepped our way inside with the tree, and though I was trying not to look at anything, the smell hit me hard. The tiny kitchen reeked of cat litter and what I could only guess was Mr. Kipling. The house was as cold as the café. Newspapers littered almost every surface. It was worse than I'd imagined. Linda began bustling about, clearing a space, searching for the box of lights, apologizing. Mr. Kipling began to whistle and chirrup from his cage like a video game on the fritz.

"Thank you, thank you so much for your help," Linda said. "Could I offer you a drink of some kind?"

She was as uncomfortable as I would have been with them in my kitchen. A thin gray cat was pawing at a green string of lights.

"I really should get going. It was a lot of fun."

She shook my hand, smiled in pained way, raised her hand to her hair. "It was, wasn't it?"

Bella followed me outside onto the front step, holding the screen door open. Her face had gone quiet. This was her house behind her, and she suddenly looked very shy. The bird let out a tremendous whistle from the kitchen.

"Mum does the best she can."

"I know she does."

I could feel the empty house waiting in the woods, the fire burnt down, the long months ahead. I needed to turn and leave, but my feet felt heavy.

"Do you think you'll go to college next year?"

"Depends on Mum. On the café. But I hope so. All those zygotes have to go somewhere, right?"

"Sure do."

"And not just in my thoughts."

A light breeze lifted at her hair. I had a sudden urge to escape with her, to drive north and to keep on driving. I pictured a roadside motel, a diner. We could join up with a circus; we could find work. She was so young, I could basically invent her, and invent myself in her eyes—we could probably stretch it until summer before it collapsed. Then there would be the conversations, the letters. The time to show my compassion.

The swiftness of the calculations was awful.

"Merry Christmas," I said.

"Merry Christmas."

She stepped back inside her house, let the screen door close. But before closing the inner door, she held up one hand to the glass pane. She held it waist-high, lightly, as though she were just reassuring herself that the glass existed. Maybe she was being dramatic again, but something about it moved me terribly.

I drove slowly back through town, then up into the woods. Dusk had fallen. The dark beyond the farmhouse didn't feel heavy, so much as something that could rise up and swallow a man. The yellow cone of light from the headlights was a thin protection. The trees were so bright inside the light, so dark beyond. It felt like other people had once been in these woods, but now they had disappeared.

The week after the party, I found myself taking more walks than usual, examining faces more closely beneath the porticoes on Via Irnerio. Wherever I went, Milena's presence felt close to me, as though I was perpetually on the verge of seeing her. Even inside the apartment, I found myself getting up from my desk at odd times, poking my head out into the stairwell, listening for footsteps or a voice. I wondered if I would recognize her voice— I couldn't remember it exactly, only the smoothness of it, the way it seemed not to interrupt the moonlight. I told myself to calm down, not to be such a daydreamer, but the feeling I'd had when we were on the roof kept coming over me, stealing between me and whatever I was trying to write. It was like distant music, sometimes louder, sometimes softer, and it stole into every gap in my day—at breakfast over my cereal, on my walks down Via Zamboni, in the evening as I came out of the shower. It was always waiting, and I desperately hoped it would turn into more than just music. I'd never felt anything like it. It seemed too persistent, too beautiful not to come closer and take form.

Juan Ignacio told me she lived upstairs, but just coming out of our apartment and looking up the drafty stairs made my heart hammer in my chest. Besides, what had started between us had started in a way that didn't follow any conventions, and I felt almost superstitious about letting it continue that way. Usually, if I liked a girl and there were signs she liked me, I was able to ask her out without hesitation. But this was entirely different. Nothing from my past seemed to apply. Since the eye accident, I hadn't had a girlfriend. Senior year, I'd dated more than ever before, but that just meant staying one step ahead of intimacy, a kind of musical chairs, so I'd never have to face myself or a woman when the music stopped. But what I'd felt on the rooftop with Milena had connected with a longing that frightened me in its intensity. Perhaps it had always been there, but it had become palpable only since the accident. I didn't know what it was made of exactly, but it had something to do with that gap between what was behind my eyes and what was outside them, and with the need to be with a woman who could make contact with both, who could make each realm as real as the other.

But as the March days wore on, and as I ate lunch with Juan Ignacio trying to pay attention to his rhapsodies about Italian women, my doubts began to grow. Had I misread our conversation? Had that softness in her eyes not been for me but just for something she was remembering about herself, that teenager in her grandmother's garden? The possibility made it difficult to eat. I'd been so certain when we said good-bye that we'd see each other again. But a week had passed. Sometimes, staring out my window late in the day, the shadows of the porticoes slanting long in the street, I knew she'd felt it, knew we'd both felt it moving below us. Maybe it had scared her for some reason. Maybe I had to go find her. But then I'd remember the two men she'd been dancing with and my stomach would catch. Maybe every man fell in love with her a little. Maybe she was out of my league. Maybe our rooftop conversation had been just a pleasant diversion for her, a minor perk in her evening.

But whatever I told myself, however I tried to slow my heart, the distant music kept on playing. Reading at night on my mattress, I came across a beautiful passage in *All the Pretty Horses*, and I imagined reading it to her, imagined how she would enjoy it. When I ate at the stand-up pizzeria on Via Irnerio, I thought of bringing her there, not to eat but just to introduce her to the stout pizza lady who called me *Caro* and always asked if I had a girl. Strangely, I was more aware of what I enjoyed—just having Milena in my thoughts somehow made my life more worthwhile, justified it in a way. My days at my desk, my afternoons walking the city, took on meaning in what I imagined to be her eyes.

But now nearly two weeks had passed since the party, and still I hadn't seen her. I steeled my courage, put on my blue button-down, the one I thought made my eyes look best, and started up the stairs. It was just dusk, not too late to go calling on her, whatever that meant, and I hit the glowing switch in the stairwell to turn on the light. I tried to clear my head, to think what I might say, and I told myself not to say too much. But as I rounded the landing between our floors, there she was.

"It is you," she said.

I nodded.

"I am just coming to knock on your door. It is this floor?"

"One floor down," I said. My voice had turned into a bird that might or might not be trained.

"But you are here?"

I didn't understand.

"You are friends with them?" She pointed to the door.

"I was coming to see you."

"But I am upstairs."

"I was on my way up."

"This is strange."

"Yes." What we were saying wasn't what we were saying.

She looked down at her feet for a moment. "You like to bicycle?"

"I don't have one here."

"But I borrow you one. Tomorrow we ride into the hills and make a picnic. I have no classes. You are free? The weather is good."

Everything waiting on my desk, everything I'd been hoping to finish the following day, didn't matter anymore.

"We leave in the morning. You have an appointment or so?"

The stairwell light buzzed off. It was on a timer. For a moment, I couldn't see her. Slowly the stairs appeared again, the shadow of the elevator grate. She was in silhouette. She rested her hand by the small orange glow on the wall, but did not press the switch.

"It is beautiful in the hills," she whispered.

"Yes?"

"You will like it. You come?"

The main door opened downstairs. The light buzzed on. I squinted, took a step back. We had been standing very close.

"Yes," I said.

"Good. Now I must go."

She turned and went nimbly up the stairs. I listened as her footsteps faded above me. I listened until there was nothing more to listen to.

The moonlight made it impossible to sleep. It washed over the window ledge and turned the floorboards and blanket ghostly white. The snow had stopped, at least for the moment, but it carried into the room with the moonlight, as though the whole room were being buried in transparent snow. It was probably two or three in the morning, but I pulled on my snowpants, my wool sweater, and climbed up to the roof. There was a wood panel at the top of the stairs—you just had to duck your head and push hard with your shoulders—and it opened into a small square room with no heat, windows on all sides, a kind of look-out tower. The windows were opaque with frost. I picked up the shovel and wedged my way out the door, the snow waist-high. The night was astonishing. The air so clean, the tang of woodsmoke from the chimney. The sky soft and oceanic, with a few thin archipelagoes of clouds. The stars didn't shimmer as austerely as against a black sky, but they seemed more at ease. The snow in front of the house was so blue, so luminous, it looked lit from below. I began shoveling, careful not to nick the tar-paper roof, stopping every now and then to look out at the woods. The snow on the trees glittered wildly, every movement of my eye returned by millions of flecked blue shimmers. The night was so quiet. The moon was watching, and the stars were watching, and the snow slid off the edge of the roof and landed quietly on the snow below. Each time I stopped to join in the watching, I had the feeling I was showing the night's beauty to someone else, sharing it with someone who understood. I shoveled the full perimeter of the roof, a thin sweat beneath my clothes. When I turned to luxuriate in the night once more, I felt a presence behind me, a hand reaching for my hand.

"It's beautiful, isn't it?" I said.

I could feel her breathing. I could feel the touch of her hand through my glove. We looked out at the strange illuminated night, at the lunar peace of it all. There was too much beauty to be able to breathe it in alone. I didn't need to turn, didn't need to see her face.

A chill caught me from behind, the hairs at the back of my neck prickled. Without any movement, the trees seemed to go naked, the night's enchantment dissolved. Again, every star, every tree, was just survival. Everything was fighting for itself. The chill stole the air from my chest, invaded my lungs. There was no one beside me. I knew I was alone.

She rode ahead of me, opening the cool Bologna morning as she went. The sky was clear blue and we rode past the women window-shopping beneath the porticoes, past the short line at the *La Repubblica* newspaper stand, past the man from the motorcycle store out in his purple jumpsuit, then left onto Via Indipendenza, her hand signaling and nearly touching an orange city bus sweeping its turn beside her, two boys in the window pointing and smiling, then the bus pulled ahead, and the street opened to its full size: banners draped above the broad avenue with announcements I didn't try to understand, the porticoes extending in classic perspective all the way down to Piazza Maggiore. Milena glanced back, said something I didn't catch. Then she rode standing again, speeding forward towards the hills as though pulled by a magnetic force. I pedaled hard to keep pace, forgetting everything but the sunlight opening on the high walls of the apartment buildings and the ease of the invitation. It had all been so simple.

As we came into Piazza Maggiore, a man's voice was spreading through the open square over a loudspeaker. We were riding side by side now, past the Neptune statue with its shooting fonts, past the city hall that looked like the keel of an old ship, and towards a small crowd gathered by the steps of the church. Beyond the church the street was cobblestoned, no porticoes, and soon we were on the outskirts of the city. Even now, as we rode, it was still going on. I'd felt it during her invitation on the stairwell and as we packed our picnic shoulder to shoulder in my kitchen. It had been more than two weeks since our conversation on the roof, but the conversation had never stopped. It had gone on without us. I told myself that was all it was, all I needed it to be—a conversation, a hum, a hue in the air. Slowly, I told myself, whatever happened, I would proceed slowly, and just let the feeling unfurl.

We turned up a very steep side street and it climbed like a vine. The pedals grew tight, and Milena smiled at me as I gave in and walked my bike beside her. Around the curve at the top of the hill, the pale yellow and burnt red houses stopped and the trees changed, leafy branches making a canopy over the edge of the road, tufted grasses high at their trunks. The road grew flat, and we rode easily again, the sun warm in flashes, the air cool in pockets, and then the dilapidated wooden fence that had been running alongside us stopped, and the trees stopped, and we rounded another bend and came out to a ridge. The hill sloped down steeply all green with the tops of the cypresses and pines, and far down below was Bologna. I'd felt so at ease, almost like we were riding bikes in my own neighborhood, and it was a wonder to remember we were in Italy. Milena nodded towards it, and I rode slowly behind her, looking down over the terra-cotta roofs pink in the distance and the Two Towers, streets radiating out from them in all directions, and Piazza Maggiore, neat and model-sized. I thought she'd stop, but she kept pedaling, and the ridge curved back into the trees, dipped into leafy shadow, then up a small rise, the trees fell away again, and when we emerged into the sunlight, I knew we were somewhere.

Milena braked and I pulled up beside her. "The park is not far," she said, breathing fast. "Just on the other side of the hill. There is a road you do not see. We eat there, no?"

I looked up to our right—long grasses and wildflowers made the land sway in the breeze. The hillside formed a broad horseshoe, or a kind of bowl, rows of apple trees, with crooked branches and small white blossoms, sloping down below us.

I nodded upwards.

"But here?" she said. "It is not a park."

A shallow ditch lined the road, and I wheeled my bike over to it and leaned one handlebar against the grassy embankment. "There's no fence."

"Naya, maybe it is OK. I think nobody comes."

She leaned her bike ahead of mine. We found a less steep place to begin the climb and started up. The soil was clumped between the grasses, the footing not so sure, and I thought to offer my hand. But I didn't know what would happen if we touched. I kept climbing. The hillside leveled into a little plateau before it rose up again, the tall grass wet with dew. We couldn't see the road and the road couldn't see us.

"Good?" she said.

We shook out the blanket from her pack and spread it on the grass. The blue heat buzzed. Back behind the bowl of apple trees, the road reemerged and curved around to the left, and above it, the green hills were hazed in sunlight.

"You enjoy life very much."

I turned. She was sitting on the blanket, her hand held to her forehead. Her eyes were shaded and very deep-set with the sun. It was strange—I'd forgotten she was there, or, really, forgotten I was there, forgotten she could see me. I didn't know why I was so at home with her. It made me uneasy.

I began to unpack the sandwiches with sun-dried tomatoes and cream cheese, the blood oranges, the bottles of water.

"Did you often make hikes as a boy?"

I shook my head. "Did you?"

"At my grandmother's house, the one I told you of, we made hikes. There are paths and huts where you stop for food or drink, and high up there are the fields with cows. We don't go often now, but I liked this very much as a girl."

"The cows are up in the hills?"

"Not in the snow or so, but high up in the hills, many cows. You can touch them. If you are soft, they do not move away."

I handed her a sandwich. I tried to do it softly.

"And you? You did not go for walks? I imagine you did this often as a boy."

"No," I said.

"But I am surprised."

"Maybe you don't know me so well."

She glanced over at me. The words had come out more sharply than I'd meant them.

"Maybe I do not," she said quietly.

"I'm sorry."

"No, you are right."

I didn't want to be right. "I hiked in the summers," I said. "At camp. But back home, during the school year, I had a different life. I was always waiting for summer to start again."

"Ya, this I understand." There was something in her voice.

"How so?"

"You ask many questions."

"So do you."

She gave me a look that was becoming familiar—a slight pout, head tilted, eyes half-closed but very bright. It said, *This is so, but you are not supposed to say it is so.* "I sit in my window sometimes at night and look at these hills. I have a glass of wine, maybe smoke a cigarette—but you do not smoke, no?"

"You're stalling," I said.

"Stalling." She looked at me, as though acting out the word. For a moment, there was only the conversation that had been riding below us, the sound of the wind in the grass. She looked away. "At night, I sit in my window and listen to music. The Sibelius violin concerto or Schubert or Schumann. And there is so much in the music, and so much outside in the night. But the next morning I must go to class. And I go, and it is interesting or so, and at night there are cocktail parties with this very small small talk. But it is important. So I go, I talk small. But I am waiting all the time. Like you said, you waited for summer and camp to start again. But for me, it is not summer. And I do not know when it comes."

We ate our sandwiches, looked out at the apple trees. "I do not know why I tell you all this," she said.

"I was beginning to wonder."

"But it is not boring and typical, these concerns of the future bourgeois?"

"You're not typical," I said.

She was quiet for a while. She was still beside me on the blanket, but she was very far away. Then the spell seemed to be broken. "Do you tell me?"

"Tell you what?"

But the way she was looking at me, her face as gentle as when she described the cows in the mountains, I knew. The breeze sifted through my bare feet, and I could hear the wind rustling in the grass. It seemed there was no one for miles. Her voice came from very close. "You tell me what happened to your eye?"

I'd seen her noticing it during our first conversation on the roof, the pupil now two years after the accident permanently dilated, one of my eyes blue, the other black. But hearing her say the words, the actual words, made my chest go hollow. People had asked before, but it had never felt like this. Usually, my body just went into lockdown, bracing not to feel anything as I answered. I'd give the facts as though I were a doctor reciting a case history. But now I could feel a kind of fault line running through my chest. I tried to keep my voice level. I gave my usual response. The basketball game, the accident, the doctor's diagnosis. How I adjusted to playing sports. How my sense of hearing grew more acute. How the pupil had dilated now, but since the eye didn't see, the change didn't really matter. I could have been telling the history of some long-forgotten country.

"But how do you see now?"

"With my other eye," I said, trying to smile.

"Naya, I know this. But the world. It looks different?"

My fault line wasn't faring well. The whole hillside seemed to be finding its way inside me, guided by her voice. "No one's ever asked me that."

"You did it to me."

"Did what?"

"Made me talk."

"Hardly."

"You're stalling. This is what you say?"

Her eyes were so ready to listen. I could feel my checkpoint guard nodding off, could feel the urge to tell her more than I should. The day had opened too wide, and I didn't want to be here, didn't like how uncertain I felt. Wouldn't I just be trying to impress her, trying to use my blindness as a way to win her heart? But I also knew if I didn't say anything, the need to talk would just keep on waiting.

"Tell me," she said.

I told myself to go slowly, to say nothing I wasn't ready to say.

"One night," I began, "when I lived up in the hills, I took the last bus back from the city center. It let me off outside

Calderino around midnight. I had to walk three kilometers in the dark, no cars on the road, the houses with no lights on. I passed the gas station, the little bar. A stream ran alongside the road, and the reflection of the moon stayed with me as I walked. I was a little nervous, a little cold, but mostly I just felt good, like I could walk anywhere."

There was so much space in the way she was listening. I knew I sounded strange, but it was the only way I could do it— to tell it as a story.

"When I finally came to my road and climbed up the gravel path, I didn't want to go inside. It didn't feel right to go inside. Everyone else was inside, already asleep. And the night had this clarity to it. The gravel white in the moonlight, a few clouds drifting by the moon. The way the town looked so quiet, the small roads, the houses. The way I knew people would get up in the morning and drive down those roads, going into Bologna to work. Life seemed to fit together. And the strange part was that my seeing that way fit together, too. Like I was a part of the town, a necessary part, kind of like a night watchman. Like someone ought to be awake in the night, not to protect the town exactly, not to scare off possible intruders or anything, but just to see the town while it slept, to be aware of it. I know it probably sounds crazy. But it seemed important somehow."

"And you stood outside for a long time?"

"It seemed like a long time. Yes."

"But then you went inside?"

Again my chest hurt. I nodded.

"But really, now, it is always like this? In some way you never go back inside. You are always outside in the night? Always watching?"

My throat felt thick. She'd understood. "Something like that."

"And it does not get cold? Always being outside?"

Her hand rested just inches from mine on the blanket. I wanted so deeply to touch it, just to feel her skin against mine.

"Do you want to read?" I said.

I pulled out the book from my backpack, strangely disappointed, as though she was the one who had stopped the conversation. It was a panic move, but it was the only thing I could think of.

I lay back on the blanket. She lay down beside me. I could smell her—the sun warm on her skin, something floral in the smell of her hair. I held the book open with my palm at the top of the page, blocking out the sun. The ground felt solid against my back, but my voice vibrated wildly in my chest. I tried to focus on the words, on the boys riding their horses across the barren plains of Mexico, the air hot and dry, but I knew beneath the page she was so close. Her arm lay just beside mine on the blanket, and I could feel her through my whole body, could feel the pull to brush my arm against hers, just to have that touch. The whole afternoon I'd felt it, the desire to be closer, physically closer, and I'd kept pushing it back, kept looking at the beauty of the hills instead of at her.

She began arranging her sweater as a pillow.

"You can put your head on my chest," I heard myself say.

Something was surprised in her eyes, genuinely surprised, but from very close. She took out the pins and her hair fell down in a soft curve by her neck. I was grateful for the book in my hand—grateful to have words ready, words that weren't mine. Then she lay down, the soft weight of her head a reassurance on my chest, her hair warm from the sun. I kept my voice reading: the boys were doing something, growing apprehensive on their horses—a gang of men was approaching from the distance, but the words were slipping back into just words. Looking below the page, I could see the nape of her neck, and I tried not to look, but then my hand was moving in her hair, the long strands silken and warm. My body was moving in a thousand directions beneath the book, but my voice kept on riding through the hot Mexican desert. Then her hand slid onto my shoulder. I turned the page. Her hand slid farther onto my shoulder, and I knew it wasn't because of the ominous men on horses in the distance. I put down the book behind my head, and she turned her face towards me. There were wisps of sunlight and then her lips.

As we kissed, her hair a soft drapery around us, there was nothing I could do. The world fell away and became deeper all at once. We were inside the scent of the long grass, inside the buzz of the heat. Inside the current of the conversation that had been going on without us, rising and falling on it, the sun carrying us on a raft of light. As I pulled her closer, as I felt her body beneath mine, there was the sense of riding with her on that current through a secret opening in the afternoon, traveling into some realm that wasn't day or night, or inside or outside, somewhere where there was no possibility of getting lost.

When we opened our eyes, far off in the apple trees, there was the call of a bird. Milena curled in by my neck. "I must hide in you."

"In me?"

"From you. With you. In you. All these things."

I tried to get her to look at me, but she kept her eyes away. "I feel too much. This is a problem," she said.

If it was a problem, it was a problem I wanted us to have. "We'll figure it out."

She sat up, stared out at the apple trees. The side of her face was a face I hadn't seen. "Naya," she said. "You do not know."

7

A truck was approaching. The sound came pushing through the gathering dark, too thick, too constant to be anything native to the woods. Nothing alive, I thought, would willingly give away its location like that. It was late afternoon, the clouds trailing purple above the pines at the edge of the field, the troughs in the snow filling like faint blue pools. I'd started taking late afternoon walks, no snowshoes, just past the apple trees, past the abandoned house, usually stopping somewhere alongside the field. I liked looking at the horizon line. The snow lay scalloped and wind-whipped like an ocean, and the sky above the darkening pines pulled on me like the horizon at the ocean, but here I could keep on walking if I wanted to—into the field, into the dimming whiteness, into the dark embrace of the trees. Sometimes I'd picture myself doing it, walking and not turning back—my own jacket clear against the snow-filled field, then a speck of color fading into the distance. It would be like walking an empty page—until there were no more words, no more letters, no more past. Or maybe some first letter would eventually start to appear on the far side of the trees, on the far side of the darkness, as though some portal opened there into another world. I didn't know if it was a fantasy of becoming visible against that emptiness, or if it was simply a fantasy of disappearing, of becoming as much a part of the land as the snowy trees. Either way, the field and the line of the distant pines had begun to hold weight for me, to exert a gravitational pull.

But the drifts in the road were no higher than my shins. There was no reason to plow. I had a sudden fear it was Bella, wearing her glittery wig, eyes fixed ahead: she'd learned to drive, borrowed a truck, and had drawn herself a little map, complete with arrows and hearts, to remember the way. It made no sense, but it was the perfect mix of fear and fantasy, of guilt and longing—my imagination abducting the girl into abducting herself. I'd looked at her too long, she'd felt what was in my head, and now she was calling on me to deliver. But as the truck nosed out of the trees, its yellow headlights playing over the snow, I recognized it immediately. The plow angled to the side, the wooden slats along the bed. I wasn't relieved, or even disappointed, as much as surprised. Nat almost never plowed this late in the day. And there wasn't much new snow to plow.

Maybe the whole Y2K thing had spooked him. I'd noticed the onslaught of exclamation marks on the magazines at the checkout line at the C&C: *Millennium Madness! Will Computers Melt Down?!? Apocalypse Now!* At that fateful tick when one millennium ended and the next refused to begin, computers everywhere were supposed to go on the fritz: planes would plummet from the sky, bank vaults would swing open, power grids would dissolve. Everything wouldn't just go dark but Dark Ages dark, and we would be thrown back into mass confusion, into the primordial terror of the dark side of the moon. To me it seemed laughable, a collective hysteria—like a grown man's horror at the prospect of losing his remote control. But maybe I should have been more understanding: after all, what was I doing in the woods but trying to come up with my own bulleted list for survival, trying to figure out what was essential for living in an altered world?

Of course, New Year's had come and gone without my even noticing—only the headlines at the C&C had changed. *Recon-*

sidering Technology, Y2K Hoax, U.S. Government Spends Three Billion Dollars to Avert What? But maybe Nat had been spooked. Or maybe he thought I had been.

He rolled up beside me now, rolled down his window. He wasn't wearing gloves or a hat. "Was in the neighborhood." He motioned with his chin as though there were houses around.

"Nice afternoon for a drive."

"Can do a little dust-up for you. No charge."

"I appreciate it."

He blew on his hands, considered the glowing tip of his cigarette. He looked like he'd been out driving for a while. The ashtray below the radio was jammed with butts. "Just wanted to tell you my son will come down."

I didn't understand.

"He's a responsible kid. A storm hits, he'll be down in a few days. Plow you out clean. He knows these parts. He'd rather sit in the house, play his video games, but I took him hunting around here when he was a kid."

He looked straight ahead, his hand still on the wheel.

"Are you going away?"

A wry smile creased his eyes. "I thought about that. Drive over to Burlington, fly all the way down to Miami. Have myself a big party on the beach. I've never seen the ocean, did you know that? Strange for a man my age."

The dashboard glowed in front of him. His skin looked faintly yellow. I could feel the road without him.

"Are you sick, Nat?"

"Docs just say take it easy for a while. Maybe a month or two. You know. One doc says one thing, another doc something else. Regular geniuses, they are."

I felt a stab of sympathetic anger. The last doctor I'd seen had paraded five med students my own age into the examining room without asking my permission, and had flashed his penlight while they took a look, one after the other, as though I were simply a jar of formaldehyde, a blind eye floating in the dark.

"What is it?" I said.

"Liver. Maybe. They don't know." He nodded towards the woods behind him. "But summer comes, I'll be here. Back in my trailer. You'll see more of me than you want."

"I'll hold you to that."

I realized I'd put my gloved hand on his door. He was my main connection to the outside world, and I was suddenly afraid to lose him. I felt the urge to put my hand on his shoulder, but it wouldn't have been right. I just gave a tap on the door, like it was an extension of his body. But even that felt strange. "Take care of yourself," I said.

"Don't let me catch you up in that hospital."

"You won't."

"Just keep eating. Keep going to town."

I thought he'd meant he didn't want me to come for visiting hours. "Promise," I said.

"You need anything, you call my wife."

"I will."

"Anything."

He gave me a last, emphatic look, and the truck rolled forward, his window still down. He seemed to be towing dusk behind him, the darkness clustering around his red taillights.

The woods went terribly quiet, the trees along the road in silhouette, tall black spires that could have been made of stone. Early evening had settled over the field like a bruise. I could still feel the pull of the horizon beyond the trees, but it shamed me now. Nat must have thought of himself as my protector, as a kind of guardian for the kid in the woods, and it hurt to realize how much he cared about me, maybe because I'd stopped thinking I meant much to anyone. And it hurt to feel how much I cared about him. I barely knew him.

His truck faded out of sight, and with the evening chill slipping through my beard, I thought of what it would mean to lose the people I did know. A few years earlier, after my grandfather's funeral, Mom had told me something Poppa had said to her when his own father had died. He'd been knotting his tie in his bedroom before the funeral, and he hadn't heard her at the door. He was soft-spoken, my Poppa, a man with a natural kindness that generally sheltered him and everyone he loved. But there was something different, something bereft in his eyes. When Mom sat down next to him on the bed, he said, "Now I know what forever means." Mom had teared up telling me the story, growing uncharacteristically quiet afterwards. We were driving from Newburgh back to Boston, and her attention didn't flick to something on the side of the road, or fall through a side door into some other story. The trees alongside the highway kept streaming by. There was only that fathomless void of what her father had felt losing his father, and of what she had felt losing hers. She apologized for crying. There was a tremendous loneliness in her, so beyond her daily concerns, which I'd never imagined she had. An otherness from everything else in the world. It wasn't that I'd still thought of her as an extension of me, the way so many children think of their mothers, but I'd assumed she still thought of me as an extension of her. Most of the time, for better or for worse, that's how she acted. But there was this other part. A part of her, because her father was waiting there, already tending towards the beyond. And I suppose it was the first time I knew, really knew, my mother would die. Her father had passed on that *forever* to her, and some day she would pass on that *forever* to me. She wouldn't be there to answer a call from the hospital, or be there for me not to call from the woods. That's what death was—no matter the love that had preceded it, there would be no answer, no possibility of an answer, forever.

As I continued walking between the tracks of Nat's truck,

the evening closing around me, I tried not to think of losing anyone in my family. I'd assumed the lives I'd left would stay the same: Mom and Dad and Matt would be just where I left them, their daily routines predictable almost to the half hour—the breakfast cereals, the commute, the evening news. But maybe it wouldn't work that way. Terrible things happened. Illnesses, accidents. And I felt irresponsible in a new way—not just because of some expected me I was abandoning but because of them, because of my responsibility to them as their son and brother. I couldn't bear the thought of Mom or Dad or Matt getting sick—especially while I was away, occupied with my own needs, so deeply unable to help. And I couldn't bear the thought of what it would mean to them if I disappeared.

Nat turned around down by the meadow, his headlights swinging back towards me through the trees. I needed to be doing something, to be fighting for something, but I didn't know for what. Or maybe I was fighting, but just too slowly.

As Nat passed, he didn't slow down, just raised one finger from the steering wheel. He hadn't lowered the plow.

There were footsteps coming down the corridor, a quick double knock, Milena peering in my room, clicking the door shut behind her, and then her hurrying across the tile floor to my mattress. She sat down beside me. She looked at me for what felt a very long time. "It is still you," she said.

She ran a finger along my cheekbone, and when I kissed her, the book I'd been reading slipped to the floor. My hand was already deep in her hair, my other hand pulling her towards me.

"But I must take off my boots."

She began to unlace them. Her shins were very white.

"You are smiling at me."

"It doesn't quite seem real."

She put my hand on her thigh. "But I am very real, no?"

The room was taking shape around us. The pile of books on the nightstand, the bedside lamp, the mattress covered by a thin blue blanket. No colorful world maps on the wall like in Juan Ignacio's room, just strips of paper with my own chicken-scratch handwriting taped above the desk, quotes stolen from Van Gogh, Chekhov, Silone—nearly all about love or art or both. So much of the room had been aspirational, something I didn't know if I could actually live by. But this was the third night Milena had come, and with her sitting there on the mattress beside me, everything felt possible.

"Class was OK?" I said.

"But do not talk now."

Clothes tangled at our feet, our bodies clear of buttons and denim and silk, clear of lace and cotton and clasps, nothing between us now, finally just hips and smoothness and heat, the bedside lamp knocked off the bedside table, and her voice very close in my ear, "But we do not make love."

In the rush, language just tiny houses and roads seen from far above, I understood her as talking not about sex but about love itself, *we do not make love*, as though she were saying love was something you couldn't make but could only find.

She'd said it every night, but now she said, "Please, do not listen to what I say," and when we were still again, her head on my chest and the room still moving, she said, "But I do not sleep here every night."

But every night she came. A few nights later, she sat facing away from me, unhooking her bra under the pajama top.

"Should I close my eyes?"

"Naya, but you must let me pretend it has only been a week."

"A week."

"Only a week since I come to you."

"But it has only been a week."

She draped her bra over her satchel, moved towards me. "This is why you must let me pretend."

Neither one of us was so good at pretending. She began to bring me things. One night, she opened her satchel and fished out disks and a portable CD player. We started with *La Bohème*. We sat with the libretto in the candlelight, looking back and forth between the Italian, the German, and the English, then not looking at the words and only listening. A group of starving artists has no money and no heat in a garret in Paris; it's a frigid Christmas Eve. There's a knock at the door—the dreaded landlord. The friends go out; Rodolfo, the writer, stays behind to finish an article he's writing; there's a second knock, and just from his response, you can hear he's going to fall in love. The knock is the same, the *who is there?* is the same, but the music lifts. It's Mimi, who lives upstairs.

Milena clutched my arm as we listened. I'd always scoffed at opera by default—it was reserved for ironical scenes in movies when the guy crashes his car, ruins the girl's new dress, bungles everything. You weren't supposed to live with such grand passions. But with Milena warm beside me, with the Bologna evening breeze playing at the sheets, the music didn't feel outsized. When Rodolfo introduces himself to Mimi—*Who am I? I'm a poet. And what do I do? I write. And how do I live? I live!*—there's no part of his life that isn't fuel for what he's singing. He's singing with his whole life, his whole past, his whole heart—all of it there in the fullness of his voice, the strings lifting with him, the feeling so much bigger than anything appropriate for meeting your upstairs neighbor, and yet entirely appropriate for the feeling of falling in love. He's giving himself to her fully, and in giving himself fully he becomes fully himself, in a way he hasn't been with his friends or his work. My skin turned electric and tears came to my eyes, and Milena made no move to wipe them away. As the aria ended, I felt as though she had returned me to some unknown part of myself, to some interior country where everything I'd felt and longed for made sense. It was similar to what came over me when I read, but now the feeling was outside of me, too—it was vibrating off the walls, off the bed, and I wasn't alone with it.

She began reading *All the Pretty Horses* on her own, sneaking it to school in her satchel among her books on European political history and global justice. At night, she'd update me on what she'd read, on where John Grady Cole and Lacy Rawlins were in their journey across Mexico, on the forbidden romance between John Grady and the Mexican girl Alejandra. I loved hearing her tell the story—the brightness in her eyes the same as when she'd told me about *Narcissus and Goldmund*—and I couldn't help hoping when she talked about John Grady and Alejandra that in some way she was talking about us. Spring had come full force into the city, bringing fruit vendors, opening the window shutters on the apartment buildings. The Giardini Margherita were full of teenagers practicing love. And night after night, we returned to each other up in my room. I didn't go to any more Hopkins parties. We ate out together rarely. We knew Juan Ignacio knew about us, but I didn't talk about it with him. It was an alternative life from the lives around us, and from the lives we had come from, but it felt possible—a different way of living, one that was guided by what we felt for each other, and sanctioned by all the quotes hanging on my wall, the opera we were listening to, the books we were reading.

Some nights she asked me to read *All the Pretty Horses* to her. Some nights she read to me in German. Some nights we didn't read or listen or talk at all. We simply got beneath the covers, the April breeze drifting through the window, the candle wavering on the tile floor.

I should have known better. I hadn't counted on the dark, how quickly it would fall. I'd sat too long, drifting on the light fading on the mountains, not noticing the heavy clouds blowing in behind the ridge. And I needed to move now. Not to rush, not to risk turning an ankle by landing hard with my snowshoe on a fallen tree, but to pole and to step, to pole and to step, deliberately and without pause. It was early February; I'd learned to gauge the wind, the warnings of the clouds. I knew better than to ignore the center dropping out of the air, the wind unmooring itself from the land. I knew better than to forget I wasn't the sky and the clouds and the snow, to forget I wasn't the weather— and that it could hurt me.

I'd descended past the shelf of land, snowshoeing down the back way, not following the regular path to the meadow. It was my shortcut. During the fall, underbrush had cluttered the back trail, but the deep snow had effectively cleared it by burying everything. There was no more trail now, but I knew the house was basically to the southeast. I just had to keep stepping, to keep poling, to keep my mind calm, my body moving. I couldn't tell if the gathering white-blue darkness came from the clouds, from the dusk coming on, or from both, but I'd reach the house more quickly this way—it was barely a mile.

A crow cried hoarsely, beat its giant wings overhead, angled itself hard against the wind. The forest was emptying. The wind thrashed in the tops of the trees. The snow swirled madly, like a school of white minnows having lost direction beneath the waves. They seemed to be swallowing my face, trying to rearrange my nose, my mouth—like the horizon I'd imagined walking towards had suddenly enveloped me. My heart raced below the booming, below the quiet between the gusts, the very marrow of the trees keening against the cold, the pulp contracting inside them. I trudged on, trying not to rush, testing for buried tree limbs with my poles. I realized I couldn't picture myself in relation to the house anymore. There wasn't a familiar landmark in sight—not a boulder, not a clearing. The woods had become general. Every direction looked the same.

If I kept moving in a wide arc to the right, at worst I'd come out above the house, somewhere by the open field. If it was full dark by then, I could find my way along the road. Even a mile of road would take no more than twenty minutes. The plan was there in my head before I could agree—like I wasn't the leader, or even part of a group, but just a straggler following behind. The toes on my right foot had hardened into something like a club. I'd worn mismatched socks and could feel the cotton one inside my boot pooled around my ankle. I was usually a boy scout about layers, but the house had gone strangely quiet in the afternoon, a quiet I could hear, and I'd hurried outside, not wanting to bother changing socks when there was only so much light left in the day. *Only so much light left in the day.* Against the snow catching in my eyes, I tried to focus on the trees ahead, to work myself into a kind of rhythm. But I was pushing too fast—not just for my body but for my vision. I didn't know how to adjust, to turn my seeing down, to compensate for the speed of the storm. The woods were going flat, into one thick wall of snow and wind. I couldn't shake the feeling of being prey, of being flushed in some direction. And as I felt myself racing downwards, the words came into my head from behind me, as though from something I was trying to outrun: *If a man falls in the forest and no one is there to hear him, does he make a sound?*

It seemed a bad joke. Fragments of poems and songs sometimes swept into my head on my walks, lines I'd never consciously learned by heart. *The woods are lovely dark and deep.* But this visitation didn't seem pleasant. Its timing was poor. The trees were losing definition, dimming into silhouette. The uneven ground hovered bluish white, like a frozen brook, pockmarked here and there by fallen branches. *If a man falls in the forest, and no one is there to hear him, does he make a sound?*

The wind pitched the slender birches like ships at sea, the sustained gusts a strange uncentered kind of wave. Clearly, the wind was hearing nothing. My tracks disappeared behind me, and I was just a shallow breath, the uncomfortable gravity of a body—an alien speck of color hurrying through the wood. The snow, the wind, the trees—they would go on with or without me, no matter the thoughts ricocheting around my head, no matter the feeling or lack of it in my heart. It seemed I'd crossed into a realm where there was no sound, where no person was supposed to go, where no human could be heard. This wasn't the dissolve into a lover, the dissolve that freed you from yourself to make you more yourself. It was nothingness. I could feel my own bones inside me, could see myself as a skeleton walking, could feel my own disappearance as a disappearance already forgotten.

The blue of the snow had thickened into gray. The gap in the trees had become consistent. At first, I thought I was imagining it, but I was suddenly on a trail, and it was widening. The old logging road. The lane to the house would become visible around a bend about a quarter mile ahead. I would get back to the house—my toes wouldn't be frostbitten. My pace slowed; the wind raged. There was nothing to do but keep walking. The road was less dark than the dark around it, the opening a relief from the bullying crowd of the forest. As I neared the crossroads, I felt an unsettling urge to turn away from the house, towards town, to keep walking until I came to the lighted sign of the Gulf station, to the jingle of the bells on the door, to some clerk behind the counter whose hello or how are you would rattle around my chest like the first coin in a beggar's cup, but I knew the walk would take far too long, and even to drive, if the car could make it out, would feel very strange. To ask someone to help you to exist, without being clear what you were asking for, seemed immoral somehow. Was there nothing else to give a person form?

Eventually, there was the open field, which I did not look at, and then my car, its trunk reassuringly solid under my glove. There was the top of the yard, the snow a dark gray lake, the house a drifting black boat hunched against the wind. There was no light in any of the windows, no light spilling onto the snow. The darkness hit me like a blow. I had imagined, without realizing it, a kind of homecoming. No one tending the fire, no one cooking dinner by the stove, but just a light in the window, the sense of returning to a home. But the house was cloaked in darkness, as though it had been absorbed by the woods, as though it had become part of the beyond as well.

There was nowhere else to go. I trudged down towards the garage. I needed to build up the fire, to make toast, to take a hot shower. To do anything small and particular. Anything human.

Milena wouldn't look at me. Vanished socks were flushed out of hiding, dust flew in the midmorning sunlight. A strand of hair hung loose by her neck. She was at the mattress, kneeling down, stripping the soft, cream-colored sheets she'd brought a week earlier. She wore an old leather purse over her shoulder, her back and arms moved very fast. She'd already stuffed her striped green pajamas, which she kept under my pillow, into her satchel. The thin blanket fell onto the floor. She tossed it back with one hand, but most of the stained mattress was still exposed.

"But you have other sheets?"

"Yes. Milena?"

"They are here. They just opened the door. They are here."

"They?"

"Otto and my father. They came on the train."

The plan was for her father to come for the weekend. Her father. That was the plan. We had celebrated her birthday together the night before, and today her father would arrive.

"My father brought him as a surprise. As a present." She was standing still now, looking right at me, but I could feel both of us moving. The moment was collapsing. There was too much weight pressing in on us from upstairs.

Juan Ignacio had warned me. Slouching in the kitchen doorway the morning of the picnic, apparently fatigued by the obviousness of it, he'd said, "C'mon, man, a woman like that, you don't think she has a man in Vienna?" And then, the first night we'd made love, she had confessed it herself. "This is a problem," she'd said, her hand still on my chest. "I should not like you this way. This should not happen." What she didn't want to happen, I was certain, was love. And so I'd trusted her hand, warm on my chest, rather than her words. I'd trusted the current between us. *I realized that when you love you must either, in your reasoning about that love, start from what is higher, more important than happiness or unhappiness, sin or virtue in their usual meaning, or you must not reason at all.* It was one of the quotations we slept below every night; it was what we were living by. We'll figure it out, I'd told her. And in the following nights, wordlessly, it seemed we had. We didn't talk about Otto. I didn't ask, she didn't offer. He existed only in the background of her stories from Vienna. They'd been classmates in law school, their families were friends; beyond that, all I knew was her pet name for him was The Chinaman: he had little body hair, was shorter than she was. She said his actual name, Otto, with deep respect, almost with fear. I didn't like how the pictures in my mind changed when she said it, how he had trouble remaining in the background as part of the group. But I knew her life with him wasn't like her nights with me. Not the way her fingers clawed into my back. Not the way she'd steal looks at me afterwards, as though she'd just been introduced to herself. It wasn't a competition between me and him. It was a competition inside of her: the life she'd been raised to live versus the life she might make on her own. She was at the same crossroads as I was, I was sure of it. And if I could just take her far enough down the path with me, far enough to see how beautiful it was, we'd make the same decision together.

"For how long? How long do they stay?" I said.

"It is only three days."

"Only?"

She said nothing. She looked more agitated than I'd ever seen her.

"Are you OK?"

"Naya, I do not know. But I must go."

Her opera CDs were still on the bedside table. Stupidly, I remembered we had only made it to Act III of *The Marriage of Figaro*. The sheets cradled in her arms looked disposable, all our nights gathered up and ready to be washed away.

"I come find you when they go."

"Will you tell him?"

Her eyes pleaded.

Then she was moving by me, the hallway overly bright with sunlight behind her, the sound of her footsteps hurrying down the corridor very loud and terribly thin.

I didn't chase after her. I only imagined running up the stone stairwell and making a scene: her father looking on stunned, her eyes begging me to stop, and Otto a very real person, with leather shoes and a high forehead, with a clean shirt he had picked out for the trip, the happiness of his birthday surprise draining from his face. The scene, I realized, was silent. Or maybe they muttered a few words of German, but English had no place. The result would be the same no matter what I said.

The stripped mattress sickened me, the *La Bohème* CD cover on the bedside table, the handsome Rodolfo with his mouth open in song. Everything I'd been so confident of was contracting. Vienna, the real Vienna, with its clean streets and dark wood bars, seemed to be invading my room. The cathedrals, the apartments, the cafés with newspapers on sticks. Her stories weren't just stories—they connected to her life, to her family, which meant to obligations, to responsibilities. The very thing I'd wanted to forget in my own life she had not forgotten in hers. *How could I have been so blind?* I was the one who saw every approaching car before it turned the corner, the one who heard every last pigeon cooing down the street. But I hadn't listened, hadn't seen. *Not paying attention.* It was the one consolation prize I was supposed to have: heightened attention was mine forever. But I hadn't used it. And now there was the chance that what I'd hidden for so long, the me she'd helped me to come home to, wouldn't be enough. She might not return. She'd left all of us—Rodolfo and Mimi, and John Grady Cole and Alejandra, and all the quotes above the desk. She'd guided me into this realm, and now she'd popped back out through a hole in the hedgerow, and gone back to her real life.

I hurried down the stairwell and slipped outside, the late April morning strangely humid. Laundry hung heavy on the lines; the heat off the parked cars wound around my ankles. I hurried down Via Mascarella, then Via Zamboni, not sure where I was going, only needing to move, hoping I would run into them, dreading I would run into them, my mind a blur of things she'd said, things she hadn't said, the smell of her still on my fingers from the night before. There was blue between the clouds, but the day had too much weight, too much quiet—it was almost noon and why weren't more people on their way to lunch? Where were the familiar patterns that were supposed to prop everyone up? Or maybe I'd forfeited my admission ticket to normalcy, maybe there was no opening in the hedgerow for me to pop back through.

I needed to keep moving, past the university, past the Feltrinelli bookstore, past the café with the red chairs—my chest was beginning to feel horribly tight, and to sit would be to allow something to catch up to me, the ache, the invisibility, the anger, and I avoided the Osteria del Orso where we'd sat over a bottle of red wine, avoided Piazza Maggiore, doubled back to avoid the side street that led into the hills. We'd made our map of Bologna together. Everything between us had carried into the streets, the porticoes, the cobblestones. Her leaving me was everywhere. Bologna was no longer mine. The streets felt like they were her friends, like they'd taken her side, and they were only humoring me. No one knew who I was, no one could keep me from being invisible. No one was sitting at mission control, maintaining contact with the watchman in the night. I'd lost the new map to myself. A way of seeing that could be a way of being—a way of living for which I could be loved. Just as I'd gotten the world solid again, with a sense of myself that actually felt true, the mirror had cracked.

I found myself hurrying towards the train station. It wasn't until the train was clicking past the cindery apartment buildings, the shadows ripping obliquely away, that I understood. It didn't matter where the train was going. It didn't matter where I slept the next three nights. I just needed to be someplace new, in some other city, beneath some other sky. Someplace where it would feel right to be lost.

The snowbanks were higher than the truck, but I could see the plumes of white powder billowing up in waves, could hear the muffled throb of the engine. It was midafternoon. I didn't know what day or what month, but I'd been down to one meal a day for too long. I hadn't been able to make it to town, had begun foraging in the bomb shelter. My snowpants didn't stay on my hips. I longed for orange juice, imagined its brightness in a glass, that first pop of sugar on my tongue—wondered if I could get scurvy, what that would mean. Elsewhere, in more southern latitudes, it was probably the middle of March. But with no promise of spring in the woods, time had turned strange. It had stalled. When the phone rang, I didn't answer. I hadn't seen Bella and Linda for more than a month. They now seemed more a dream than actual people. I hadn't told Lev whether I'd stay another year, hadn't felt capable of thinking about it. Time wasn't marching forward. Days slipped into yesterday, tomorrow. The sun wasn't arcing any higher above the trees. Some days I couldn't remember anything about the day before other than the food. With the sky gone livid and skyless, the snow still falling, it was the clearest way of marking time. I'd burned through the wood supply on one side of the garage, the wall's wood slats strangely barren. Sometimes, gathering logs for the morning fire, I felt like I was seeing inside my own stomach, fuel stores running down.

I snowshoed across the meadow towards the plumes of powder, but as I pushed down the edge of the snowbank, something strange happened. I fell into a kind of time warp. Nat's head inside the cab was a bowl of sandy hair, the skin by his eyes unlined. His cigarette dangled above the steering wheel, but his face was harder. Which suddenly made me feel older—or, really, like I could be any age, like time had become the time win a dream. Then he glanced at me, scowled as he raised one hand, and I realized it was Nat's son. I wasn't sure if I preferred the dream. The son looked like Nat minus the wisdom, minus the humor. I came closer, waited, wanted to ask if Nat was in the hospital. I wanted to know when he would return. But his son wasn't interested in stopping. He slammed forward, slammed back. Muffled guitars blared from his radio, his window closed.

Then he raised just a finger, quickly, as though I might be contagious, and headed back out towards the road.

He hadn't done as clean a job of it as his father would have, but the road was functional, there was passage, a bobsled run for a car. It was probably April. There was a decent chance the last big snows had passed, that I'd made it to the threshold of spring. I would soon be able to come and go freely. I could get orange juice. And frozen pizza. The bizarre party in the aisles of the C&C would welcome me back. Maybe I'd even visit Linda and Bella at the café.

But as I clomped into the cleared lane on my snowshoes, the ground frozen hard beneath me, I turned towards the house. The smooth white alley trailed off into the deep snow past my car, into my own snowshoe prints going back and forth. That was the direction I knew. That was where I was comfortable. I didn't want to admit it, but I could feel it in my body. There was a bird-like lightness in my bones. I was still as insubstantial as the way I saw. My sense of myself was still too fragile. There was something I'd found here, something in the silence, but I didn't know how to offer it to anyone. And I didn't know how to receive anything from anyone either. I didn't know how to return. And I couldn't help seeing the cleared lane as leading farther into the woods, and deeper into winter, rather than back into town.

That afternoon I called Lev and told him I would stay.

PART III

The Point of Vanishing

8

Summer was an escape route, a perfectly open window, an excuse to leave if I wanted one. But the world had turned green again. The dirt roads were dirt roads: dusty and solid, swarmed on either side by leafy ferns, wild flowers, high swatches of grass, the grass itself swarming and clicking with legions of dragon flies, grasshoppers, mosquitoes. Deer stole through the trees. Red-winged blackbirds sang from the fenceposts. Ghost-white butterflies flitted in the heat. The green was a revelation, a prodigal son—a color that had once existed, gone missing in the snows, and miraculously returned. It opened itself through the hazed meadows, through the blue-green hills, through the reflections in the pewter green ponds; it deepened the blue in the pines, gilded the light off the streams, and relented only towards dusk, yielding to the slow antics of the fireflies, to the stars overhead, to flashes that felt like after-shimmers of the green, green days.

It made staying feel like a conviction. The surrounding promise that had tormented me during mud season—the purple branchlets of the birches, the pointed, brick-brown buds of the sugar maples, the scent of the wet earth returning to the air, every tree pushing into itself, into particular branches, into particular leaves, saying *here* and *here* and *here*—had finally come true. To stand and breathe amid that force, to feel it fighting into life all around me, had been quietly terrifying in May, as though I were falling behind while everything around me pushed ahead. As though the woods were planning a grand excursion, but I'd failed to do the necessary work to join, as though I'd been preparing nothing, while all winter the trees had been secretly storing up strength, making plans. It wasn't that I'd exactly caught up now. There were no leaves suddenly springing from my mouth, from my hands. But somehow every view in the woods had become interior. There were no sight lines through the trees; the foliage was far too thick. There was no more far away. No more complexity of depth perception, of inner and outer, of where I fit in. The world was leafy, palpable, and the fragrance of the sun on the pine needles gave shape to the air. It had a density that held me in place. The sunlight charged through my blood. I was barefoot again, wild, and some days I didn't wear clothes at all. My legs bore red lashes from the nettles. My feet were the color of the earth. I stopped using the bathroom in the house. Leaves and twigs nested in my hair. This was progress. I was becoming more fertile. My body was becoming strong. The earth was rising into me. I found myself doing push-ups, sit-ups, and I'd lie back in the meadow soaked with sweat. In winter, I'd felt almost no sex drive, but sometimes now it filled me to my very toes, a thrumming, a light inside my body, especially early in the morning, and I'd hurry outside, as though to a lover, the dewy grass cold and sharp on my back. When I exploded, my whole body flooded into the day. As I crossed the meadow back to the house, thick grass would grasp at my calves. The world was reaching for me—and I could feel myself reaching back.

But now it was October again. The green was mostly gone. Even the high grasses along the dirt road had dulled, stooping with age. The autumnal winds rinsed through the leaves, shaking the yellow birches like castanets, the air taut and crisp, as though wires connected to the sun had tightened their hold on the earth. And beneath the winds, beneath the diversionary scuffle, the land had grown quiet. No more hum and whine of insects, no more birdsong drifting through the sunlit ferns. It was like the dense quiet of a library, every occupant huddled over his own preparations, not to be disturbed. The obsessive woodpecker hammering for grubs, the squirrel gathering his winter cache. Even the quiet in the house felt different. The way the sun angled across the floorboards. The ashy breath of the woodstove. The air was too still, like a sickroom. The year before, everything had been new. My search was underway. The great epiphany felt possible, close at hand. The seasons were lining up to deliver their unforeseeable presents—the white expanse of winter, the muddy fight into spring, the glorious green summer. But now the carousel had gone round a full turn. And there was no magic billboard halfway around with an answer inscribed in luminous letters. I wondered if my search was nothing but an escape. Not an unrelenting drive to get down to the bottom of things, to some truth beyond which there was nothing greater, but simply an enormous white flag in disguise. Maybe it was a forfeit. A way to never have to speak. Not a constant prayer. Not a miracle in slow motion, but a slow-motion death.

And yet, as the nights grew chill and the approach of winter became a rumor in the air, there were signs of progress. Or, to be more precise, one sign. It came in a phone call late on a Sunday afternoon. Outside, a cold drizzle was peppering the leaves. The sound of the refrigerator humming on, humming off, had already been a full conversation. I sat waiting, as though if I sat still enough, the ringing wouldn't see me. I didn't want to interrupt my meal. The textures had become spatial in my mouth, a village I was visiting—the grains of the bread were low stone walls, the honey glimmers of sunlight off a stream.

The phone stopped ringing, then started up again. My village withered into a hill town in an old postcard, a memory I couldn't quite recollect. It was a ghost town now, the ringing a plague that had driven everyone away.

"Hello."

"May I speak with Howie, please?"

"Ray, it's me. Who else would it be?"

I was already settling myself on the daybed beside the phone. It was a wooden bench with a thin mattress, which was covered by a green flannel sheet. I sat cross-legged, my back against the wall, the high long windows to the woods in front of me. The phone hummed. I forgot I was supposed to speak. I was just looking at Ray in my mind, getting used to the pleasure of being with him.

"How's the weather up there?" he said.

It wasn't small talk. Ray had spent summers during college as a camp counselor in New Hampshire, only about ten miles from Camp Walt Whitman. We'd hiked the same mountains, camped at the same campgrounds, known the same pine trees and mosquitoes and lakes. But Ray had grown up in the hills outside San Francisco, in Lafayette—with the grass turning to straw in summer, with regular hikes among the redwoods in Muir Woods, with the ocean meaning the Pacific. As much as he'd enjoyed his summers in the White Mountains, the vistas there weren't his vistas—not the palette, not the scale, not the smell of the air. And since graduation it had been on his mind. Nearly all his college and med school friends lived on the east coast, most of them in New York City. How much did your hometown, he often seemed to be asking, the place where your senses first gripped the world, really matter? And, though he didn't quite put it this way, how much did your friends?

I told him about the leaves changing, their colors in the different weathers. I told him about my walk that morning in the rain, the mist rising from the meadow. I had the feeling I was telling him something personal. But as my mind passed by the stump from the pine sapling I'd cut for Linda and Bella, I didn't mention it. How could I explain, and to my most moral friend, that I felt virtuous for ignoring a seventeen-year-old girl and her mother? In August, I'd seen a flyer at the C&C for a jazz concert in Burlington, and I'd asked Bella if she wanted to go. I'd told myself I was asking her for the right reasons, as a kind of educational field trip, a summer celebration, and not because I was nervous to go alone, or because of the way she looked in her jean shorts and halter shirt, or because my desire for the early morning meadow was spilling over into town. Linda had said she needed Bella at the café, there was too much work, and when Bella pointed out that some afternoons they had no customers at all, Linda, her mouth twisted between anger and a terrible instinct to please, simply said, "Case closed." In my mind, ceasing to visit the restaurant had been to my credit, but just the prospect of mentioning it to Ray made me uneasy. Something didn't add up. Some unseen evidence was assembled against me. Even in my mind, it was becoming harder to articulate what I was searching for, and how I might succeed. It had something to do with the question of instincts—the right ones to follow, the right ones to ignore.

"How's New York City?" I said, finally. "What do you see out your window?"

"I'm looking at the Hudson. That's kind of nature, isn't it? The sun sets over New Jersey and the water picks up the light. But my window is dirty, and it doesn't open—so there's no way to clean it."

I wondered about myself, about being a window not opening. I wondered about what I wasn't letting in.

"I did go for a long walk a few weeks ago around Central Park. It was a clear fall day, lots of people out walking and jogging. There had to be twenty thousand people in the park. Anyway, walking back I couldn't help noticing all the dog shit on the sidewalk on Amsterdam and the smell of urine. The dogs have to go somewhere, but the urine just sits there until it rains, or until it's absorbed into the sidewalk. It's really kind of gross. I don't know why I'm telling you all this."

I'd been picturing the grime on his window, the sunset over the river, the brown stone wall around Central Park, the grass and roller skaters and joggers and pretzel vendors, and the sidewalk on Amsterdam, a street I didn't know but pictured all the same, a narrow canyon below skyscrapers. I just wanted him to keep on talking. "Go ahead," I said.

Ray exhaled deeply. "I wanted to talk to you about something."

I'd forgotten about his notorious preambles. Sometimes when we were playing cards and Ray began a story, Alexis would point an imaginary remote control at him and mime fast-forwarding to the point. "You're not worried about me again, are you?"

"I don't know where all that came from." He'd given me a phone lecture during the summer about the need to contribute to society. He'd cited sources. "I think that had more to do with my doubts than it had to do with you." He didn't sound convinced.

"That's OK."

"But I guess that's what I wanted to talk to you about."

"Your doubts?"

"Sort of."

"Go ahead, Ray. I'm listening."

"Well, we have gross anatomy lab on Thursday. It's a mandatory class. The lab is up on the fourteenth floor, and through the windows you can see people waiting at the bus stop for the cross-town bus, pedestrians going to lunch. So my group has an obese middle-aged woman. We were on her hand. It shouldn't have been anything strange. We've been dissecting her for weeks. We've done the back and the spine and the thorax. We've done the brain and the face. I've had hard days, but for the most part you just go over to this other side. It's a fascinating machine, the body, and it's easy to see it that way." He paused. "But for some reason the hand—it was her hand, a woman's hand. And I just started to feel nauseated. I had to excuse myself. At the water fountain in the hall, my autonomic nervous system was going crazy. I remembered a fetus starts with its fingers webbed, and cells have to die for the hand to individuate into fingers. I remembered how I kept looking at people's hands after learning that. I felt like I wanted to get on my knees and apologize for something. I don't even really know for what."

Ray fell quiet. The line went on buzzing. I felt a vestige of the instinct to say something, to reassure him, but the instinct was too far away. I'd been picturing everything he was saying— picturing him there among the cadavers in his white lab coat, the city going on outside with buses and people fourteen stories below. I stared at the birch tree out the window, a sodden feather of bark tattering in the wind. It seemed a reminder of the chickadees—a reminder not to hunt for what Ray was saying but just to let my mind's eye go soft, to wait until there was movement in the picture. Then I noticed something. The cadavers and the students in white coats had one kind of light on them, and the buses and pedestrians and Ray had another. It wasn't that Ray was standing in bright sunlight, nothing heavenly or weird, but just as though some movie director had been shooting the whole scene with Ray in a more natural light than the anatomy lab, shooting him according to the feeling in his voice. And the obese woman's hand—it was lit with the sunlight, too, puffy and human, but the rest of her body, which was dried and purplish, didn't look human at all.

"It sounds like two different worlds," I said.

"What do you mean?"

I told him what I was picturing.

"That's it," he said. Then he added, "You know, when I walk around the city, sometimes I feel there are different sets of rules everywhere. Sometimes even block to block. I know this sounds weird, but the city can feel like a science fiction movie. All these different dimensions. With the upscale stores on Fifth Avenue and the homeless people in garbage bags. The Upper West Side matrons and the cab drivers from Bangladesh. It just keeps changing. And changing. The values, the expectations. It makes me think of portals and worm holes, except you just have to walk and you keep passing through them. And the rules keep changing as you do. You can feel it. And I don't know which rules are mine."

I was still looking out the window at the birch tree, the rain slanting in the wind, but it felt like Ray and I were somewhere together—on those throbbing and changing streets but also suspended somewhere beyond them, in a realm where the rules didn't change, where they were universal instead of relative. Where the people and restaurants and stores still changed block to block, but where you couldn't help recognizing, where *everyone* couldn't help recognizing, the stars wheeling overhead, and the seasons following one after the next, and some center inside all of it abiding, enduring, staying the same.

"So, any advice for a poor city dweller? I mean, what have you found up there?"

I glanced at my plate on the table, my city of honeyed streams and multigrain walls. I wasn't sure if I was a fool or a prophet. "I wish I could answer, Ray."

"Nothing?"

"Really, I wish I could translate it. But I don't know how."

"Maybe once you get back," he said gently.

"Maybe," I said. And for the first time in a long time, I believed it. The rain and the glistening leaves out the window weren't just filled with shadow. I really was learning something—how to see, how to listen. I was learning how to move from the visible world to the invisible, and back again, which wasn't a helpful skill just with chickadees but with people. I'd heard something profound in Ray—his loneliness, his lostness—and my own loneliness and lostness didn't feel so strange.

"Good talking to you," Ray said before we hung up.

"Good talking to you, too."

The phone calls had grown quietly desperate. The children of Mom and Dad's friends were off to law school and new jobs, off to roommates and new cities. Phases weren't supposed to last more than a year. Dad wasn't just asking about the Honda anymore. He wanted to know about money, about plans, about my future—questions, it was clear, he'd been holding in for a very long time. My answers set new marks for evasiveness. Mom just pleaded for a visit. Family meant showing up, she said. Thanksgiving was coming. I hadn't come last year on the annual pilgrimage to Newburgh. Everyone was asking for me. My cousins Susan and Melissa. My aunt Betty. Matt. It would mean the world to Mom, just the world. She'd make the forest torte cake, just like always. I thought she was making a pun about the forest—the picture in my mind was of a cake studded with pine trees, their needles sparkling festively. But she said no, your favorite cake, the forest torte, the cake you love.

On the November night I called to say yes, expecting to receive a warm hug from Mom's voice, she responded with a stampede of questions: "Should I pick up an extra dozen bagels at Rein's? You want a frozen chocolate chip sour cream cake? You have good shoes? Dad could pack an extra pair. He could pack a tie. We'll have enough ruggelach to sink a ship, so what does it matter a few more things? As long as Dad remembers to pack them. So you have a belt? You have a comb?"

I felt as though she'd backed her car in through the woods, pushed the table out of the way, and emptied the contents of a thousand closets onto the floor. I was seeing too much, seeing things I didn't know how to see. The frame was all wrong.

But in the chill, rainy days after our call, I knew it would be different in person. In person, she'd see my eyes, she'd feel the love coming out of me. My quiet would help quiet her. I took long walks beneath the barren trees with imaginary, beautiful conversations running through my mind, conversations filled with deep understanding. Jokes with my cousin Scott; earnest questions from Melissa by the fire; maybe a football toss with Matt, the ball carrying things between us that we couldn't say. Everything I'd learned over the winter, and everything I'd felt during the summer, all that silence and vitality and love, would be like a green medallion glowing from my chest. It would emanate from my eyes. They would feel it even in my silence as I stood by the sink, or as I brought someone a piece of pie. That green glowing light would bring out a similar glow from them, and we'd bathe together in it as though in firelight. I'd always loved Thanksgiving. That feeling that there was no other place anyone in the family was supposed to be.

Leaving the house meant draining the pipes of water, pouring antifreeze into the toilet bowl. It meant finding the key so I could lock the door. It meant the excitement of travel, of going far away. Which meant packing my old duffel bag, the same bag I'd packed again and again as I'd driven around the country.

As I pulled the heavy green canvas down from the plywood shelf in my room, its musty smell carried a familiar promise. The year after Bologna, when I was desperate for some town or vista that might feel like home, it had been my faithful companion. The letters from Milena, which initially had seemed to offer a second chance, had stopped coming. Her grandmother died that July; her family needed her. I stood on a kitchen chair in my Cambridge apartment during our last phone conversation, then on the kitchen table, as though I might climb high enough to be heard. I charmed, I cajoled, I pleaded. After Otto's visit in Bologna, we'd spent one more month together, arguing, always arguing. She'd said she could not invent her life; I'd said her life in Vienna was an invention. There were tears, there were apologies. There was staggering sex. One night, we even drove to her grandmother's house in Austria. She had borrowed a car, and we drove in the night past Verona, Venezia, across the border, then up into the mountains, through tunnels and forests, until we were there by the lake where she had read *Narcissus and Goldmund* as a girl. Her grandmother was in Vienna, there was a key hidden above the lintel in the garden shed. After sleeping until midday, eating lunch, and talking very little, we started back to Bologna, but she asked me to pull over at one of the switchbacks leading down from her grandmother's house. It was a tiny church. The gravel crunched under our feet. We were not holding hands. To the left of her grandfather's tombstone was a black marble plaque. There were swastikas at the two corners, where decorative roses might have been. Our reflections were dimly visible over the names.

"My great-uncle is there," she said. "Many men from his village were taken into the war."

I had never thought of Nazis dying.

"His unit was sent to the Russian front. Within two months he was killed. His picture was on the piano when I was a girl. A handsome young man. But I am sorry. Your family. I did not think."

I didn't say anything. I was aware of the space between our hands. I didn't know whether to trust her or whether she'd brought me here to make a point. But it hardly mattered: she was right. She came from somewhere and it was not where I came from. Our pasts and our families were part of us. She could not leave hers and I could not leave mine. I looked at the names on the hard black plaque, so many names written across our bodies and our faces. That history was a part of who we were, but it horrified me to think that it was only who we were, that it determined everything.

The fall after my return from Bologna, Milena took a job at the United Nations in New York City. All summer I'd written her long, unfortunate love letters, pleading with her, citing Kierkegaard's knight of faith, quoting Chekhov's stories, writing her that we needed to follow our love, telling her it dwarfed our families, our histories, every line that surrounded us. She wrote back with more and more German in her letters, as if to share more of herself and offer less of herself at the same time. *Vielleicht in ein anderen leben. Trotz allem, hast du keine ahnung was es fur mich bedeutet dich fer kennen.* I went to the public library to look up the German, to have my heart broken again, piece by piece, by the yellowed pages of the dictionary. *Perhaps in another life. In spite of everything, you have no idea what it means for me to know you.* She'd even flown to meet me in Arizona on my drive west, and implored me, as we said good-bye in the airport, not to change, she could not follow me, but please, to live this way for both of us. When I visited her in New York City, in an effort to convince her I had more to offer than just books and opera and hikes in the desert, we went with Ray one night to the Carnegie Deli. But it changed nothing. Nothing worked.

And nothing from my old life was working either. Everything in Cambridge, where I'd taken a job as a teaching fellow, had turned foreign. The meetings with the khakis and the niceties and the proposed topics for discussion. The grad students who read every book as an argument for or against their pet theories. The family restaurants in the Square that had been overtaken by chains. The ads on the subway kiosk that featured life-size photographs of Albert Einstein and Pablo Picasso, the words *think different* emblazoned beside a little white apple, as though Einstein and Picasso had time-traveled to 1999 and derived their genius from a computer, as though the gateway to a unique way of seeing was looking at the world through a screen. I felt like a wild animal who'd mistakenly wandered into the zoo. A born believer who'd wandered into a culture of heretics.

So, after saving enough money, I'd criss-crossed the country twice, living for a few months in New Mexico, in Idaho, in Montana. I'd lived in a trailer, in cabins, in my tent. I'd woken to different trees, different campgrounds. The land kept unscrolling, the road led out to distant colors, and the big sky promised enough space for me to heal. I'd assumed visibility would have to get better—I'd find a reflection of myself in that sky, in the land, a reflection that couldn't be broken. But nothing became any clearer. Between my two cross-country drives, I returned to Harvard to work again, to cover my expenses. Mom and Dad were still proud. The golden boy trajectory appeared intact. Outwardly, I was still living that life—and my "drives" could be forgiven as eccentricity. But they were the only part of my life that felt real. Back in my apartment on Ellery Street, I was miserable, unbearable to myself. I was still leading a double life. I was impersonating my former self and not even doing a good job of it.

But now, as I packed my green duffel, I was confident I'd put in the time, endured the solitude. I'd sat with myself day after day, night after night, alone. I could already feel the green medallion glowing in my chest. I could already feel the love I would share with my family. I wasn't packing to run across the country, to search for some new horizon, but to have a preview of my return. To test what I'd learned—and what I might be able to offer.

———

The first cop pulled me over before I was out of Vermont. Or, really, I should say pulled up behind me, as I was already pulled over and already out of my car. I was at a rest stop, standing on the skirt of grass by the angled parking spaces, facing the granite wall that had been dynamited to make the highway. The rest stop had no restrooms. It had no access to the woods. From my posture—feet shoulder-width apart, hands in front of me—my reason for taking in the scenery was fairly obvious. I'd heard a car pull up, a door opening and closing, followed by a lack of footsteps. I finished, zipped up, and turned around.

"This isn't a public restroom."

It sure didn't feel very private.

"Women and children stop here sometimes. They don't want to see that."

Did he want to see that? Is that why his fender had almost hit my calves?

"Do you hear what I'm saying to you? Respond verbally if you can."

He looked to be about twenty. The only shadow on his jaw was from the brim of his trooper's hat worn low over his eyes. "I can hear you just fine," I said.

"When was the last time you did drugs?"

"Sir?"

"The last time you did drugs. Are you on drugs right now?" He shifted his weight. He was staring at my eyes. It felt like a sucker punch. A migraine was thickening behind my right eyeball.

"Not since I was in college."

"Are you sure about that?"

"I'm sure."

"And you're feeling OK?"

"Sir?"

"Are you feeling OK? Are you sick?"

"I have a headache."

"And what's that from?"

"Sir?"

"The headache. What's that from?"

"Driving. I'm driving to New York. I guess I'm nervous to see my family."

His eyes locked onto mine again. He'd probably watched too many cop shows. Had my eye, which was probably a little bloodshot, issued him a search warrant?

He glanced down, adjusted the brim of his trooper's hat. "Family makes me nervous, too. That's understandable."

I waited. His car was still running.

"Well, happy Thanksgiving. And next time make sure you find the appropriate facilities."

After he pulled out, I got back in the car and sat for a few minutes. Then I drove very slowly south towards the Massachusetts border, past the highway farms, the blue silos and fields, as though reduced speed might put the world in order. Did my eye really look that weird? Granted, it had been through some changes. First there was the accident, and the strangeness of my eye looking the same as it always had; then my pupil dilated permanently while I was in Bologna; then there were calcium deposits that flaked off on my second drive West. My eye teared through Arizona, Utah, Colorado, Wyoming, and by the time I hit the Badlands of South Dakota, it was watering steadily. I was driving with a tissue in my hand, like a woman weeping, and given the otherworldly sandstone spires, the blinding blue sky, I could have passed for a character in a sci-fi movie, a survivor of an earth destroyed. The irritation, I learned from a doctor in Minnesota, was caused by calcium deposits. "They formed on your iris there. Little pieces are flaking into the eye. Kind of like paint peeling off a fence. That's why you've got the irritation, the crying. Unless those bands are surgically removed, you can bet that irritation's going to persist." Back in Boston, I returned to Mass Eye and Ear, and a surgeon put me under general anaesthetic and chipped away, as though my eye were an ill-formed statue. The pain waited until the next morning. Beneath the bandage, which was a large white patch taped to my forehead, my eye razored with every blink, as if the red string on a Band-Aid had been dangling from my iris and someone had pulled. I was back in my childhood bedroom, below the basketball posters and the trophies, back where I'd been the morning after the accident. I knew I had to do something. I knew I had to change. No more looking for some beautiful woman or some beautiful town to save me. I needed to go far enough back so there would be nothing else waiting behind. No further layer that was just a scrim, no more version of reality that was only provisional. I had to touch the hard edge of reality, and begin from there. A few weeks later, as if to make sure I'd gotten the message, a cataract started to form on my right eye. A pearly shine, like the glint in an animated character's eye. A few months after that, I was in northern Vermont, posting my handwritten signs on the bulletin board outside the C&C. *Wanted: a cabin or house set in the woods, with good light, very solitary.*

Maybe I'd have to keep dealing with people like the cop, maybe my eye had become its own carnival attraction. I hadn't looked at a mirror in more than a year. A reflection slid over the car windows in the C&C parking lot, it loomed up in the freezer doors, it hovered in the mirror above the sink. But I had no idea how I looked, no idea what my family might see. The rearview mirror was right there, right beside me, its narrow, impartial eye open and ready, but the prospect frightened me. It had taken so long to live without a face, to live without anyone to put on a face for, and the slim mirror threatened like a cage. I didn't want to resign that freedom. I didn't want to start fitting whatever waited in the mirror into a mask.

The fist tightened behind my eye as I drove through western Massachusetts, dropped into Connecticut, and then was funneled through the narrow highway lanes of Hartford, shunted along like a bottle on an assembly line. Billboards with enormous faces of newscasters swarmed above me, their smiles desperate with dependability, one woman's glossy red lipstick strangely pornographic. The buildings kept multiplying, their regimented windows like the multifaceted eyes of insects. The colors did not make sense. The geometry was all wrong. Seeing this way reminded me of my drive west, the way cities would rise out of the desert like alien encampments, except now I wasn't a traveler from afar, not a stranger in a strange land. I'd driven this stretch of road so many times before, but it seemed the distance had become a part of my vision—it traveled with me now.

As I crossed the border into New York—*Welcome to the Empire State*—I tried to remind myself of how much I'd always enjoyed Thanksgiving. As a kid, going to Newburgh had felt like returning to the motherland. All Mom and Dad's stories took place there. Every house was a house where something had happened, every street a street that led into the past. On our annual pilgrimage, we'd troll the neighborhoods, Mom reeling up memory after memory, pointing out the house her father built on Liberty Street—*he knew where every nail was in that house*—and the house where Poppa had stood guard at the intersection, so she and her sister could sled down the street, and where she'd fallen off the front step one day and bumped her head. She'd turn in the passenger seat and show Matt and me the small bump just below her hairline, and she'd take my hand and run my two fingers over it so I could feel it. It always astounded me—looking at those concrete steps and feeling that bump on Mom's forehead, feeling time right there under my fingertips, the way something that had happened decades ago was still a part of Mom's face, still a part of who she was. "Every door was open to me," Mom would go on. "At lunch I could walk in any door—the Levinsons', or Aunt May's, or the Siegels'—and someone would be there to give me a BLT." Dad would steer the car slowly. Sometimes Mom would start to cry. "It was just different then." Dad would pat her on the knee. They never seemed as in love as they did on those drives. And I loved being part of that feeling, even if it was only from the backseat. I loved feeling that those streets and houses mattered, and that we belonged to them, or that at least Mom and Dad once had. We couldn't go into the diner without being treated like minor celebrities. Before the waitress had delivered the commandment-size menus, Mom would explain: "That woman with the blue eye-shadow, she had a crush on Dad in high school; that kind old man at the counter, he was Dad's basketball coach at the JCC; remember the story Poppa told about his teacher with the dead arm?"—then she'd imitate it, holding her arm, swinging it, "Friedman, out of here"—"That woman who was at the door, she's his daughter."

Of course, this year Thanksgiving wasn't being held in Newburgh. There'd been a change of plans. We were all going to Armonk, to my cousin Susan's house. Mom had withheld the information until our last phone conversation. Susan and Dirk's house had so much more room, she said.

"Armonk, this is the house with the twenty-two TVs?"

"It'll be fine."

"Do they have twenty-two rooms?"

"We'll sleep in Newburgh. It'll be fine. Everyone's so excited you're coming!"

Off the highway, I followed beneath the skeletal November trees into the dark heart of the suburbs. Armonk had street signs on every corner, traffic lights overhead, boutique stores with clever names. The crosswalks blazed with precision. The sidewalk was immaculate. I wondered if people were nervous to walk there for fear of feeling like blemishes. Nothing was accidental, or if it was, it was because someone hadn't done his job. A mother and daughter crossed at a perfect right angle to the car at a determined jog/walk pace—the girl in a short black dress, the mother in a pink warm-up suit. Maybe as a joke they'd limited themselves to each other's closets. Beyond them, the street was empty, everyone probably already with their families. I appreciated the quiet. There were so many pizza places. *Fresh Delicious Pizza!* And Chinese restaurants. *Daily Lunch Buffet!* Despite myself, my mouth was beginning to water. *Enjoy Coca-Cola!*

Off the main road, the houses retreated deeper and deeper on their lawns, a patch of trees adorning them here and there like a sprig of parsley. It looked make-believe—the driveways, the hedges, the box lawns—as though I was driving down a black crayon road in a child's drawing. But as the land opened beyond the first clusters of houses, it was beautiful: rolling hills thick with massive oaks, the narrow road curving sharply around jutting pudding stone. I told myself to keep seeing it that way, to keep seeing the land below everything—and to remember to do that with my family, too, to look for what glowed inside each of them, below the jewelry, the makeup, the small talk about football or the stock market. I told myself the subtext below every conversation, whatever the words were, was really love. I told myself to remember that—to bring the love I'd felt in the woods to them, to bring it in human form. My migraine was burning off. I was remembering why I had come. Granted, a nervous static was making the green medallion inside my chest hard to feel, but I trusted it was only static.

After a series of turns, I came to what Mom had described as a *new development*. Enormous houses followed a long horseshoe curve. Most of the oaks and elms had been cut down, leav-

ing the street strangely airy. Each house had a security gate, an
intercom device, a long flat driveway. There were no cars on the
road, no children, nobody on the football-field size lawns. It
seemed like a museum of houses. Some had two chimneys, others had three. Some were all brick, others a combination of
brick and wood. One house, clearly the rebel, was canary yellow.
As I kept driving, everything so new—newly painted, newly ma-
soned, newly mown—the neighborhood began to look more
like a catalogue. At the bottom right of every immense lawn,
there might have been little bars suggesting other available options. I drove at a walking pace, hoping the extra time would
help me acclimate, hoping it would diminish whatever baffle-
ment was behind my eyes.

The security gate was open, and I drove down the long
driveway, pulled in beside Dad's black Acura. Seeing it unhinged
something in my chest. It was so familiar. A hanger with cello-
phane wrap from the Chestnut Hill Cleaners hung in the backseat. A Harvard decal still adorned the back window. It had
carried them here. Mom and Dad were inside the house. Matt
and Jami's car was there, too. I would walk up the front walk,
someone would open the door, and they would all be inside. My
chest felt fluttery, my arms and legs overly alert. As though I
were about to walk onto a brightly lit stage, as though thousands
of eyes were about to see me.

I'd hardly pressed the doorbell when the white door swung
open. Everyone was gathered in the foyer. The house was so
cavernous maybe no one had wanted to get lost. Or maybe Matt
and Jami had just arrived. The floor was black and white marble
squares, everyone a chess piece. Behind them, a bronze urn of
spiky flowers sat on a pedestal. A spiral staircase swept up towards unknown splendor. My cousin Scott had opened the
door. In high school we'd looked alike, and he'd struck me as
a more normal version of myself. He'd given me my first fake

ID, taken me to my first bar, made sure I had a bottle of beer in my hand.

"Look, everyone," he said, announcing me, "it's the Unabomber!"

Smiles were slightly blurred. Mom stepped forward, kissed me on the cheek, then touched my face, as though to make sure it was real. There wasn't enough room behind me to step away.

"So hairy," she said.

Dad patted me on the back, stood too close, asked about the traffic. Matt's eyes were like a dog brushing at my pantlegs, trying to herd me back into the person he recognized. Everyone was still waiting for a clever response, a reassuring response.

"Happy Thanksgiving," I said, but my voice sounded underwater. Everyone else stood on dry land, far above me, in a greenish wavering light. More hugs followed. I was a mystery package to be held, shaken, assayed, so they might guess what was inside. Even my cousin Melissa, who came up only to my shoulder, felt too big, too close, her skin and clothing overly fragrant. Dirk's arms were as thick as a bear's. Susan's high heels sounded like gunshots down the corridor. These were woods I didn't understand. At the first chance that presented itself, I retreated to the bathroom.

It was like eating inside a pinball machine, the metallic ball shooting and ricocheting, signs lighting up and spinning for reasons I didn't understand. I was still picturing myself in front of the woodstove and trying to answer Scott's question about missing television, and then there was another question, then another. Everyone's plates filled and emptied and filled again. They all seemed to have ten minds and ten arms, the cranberry sauce and stuffing and sweet potatoes shuttled this way and that, the conversation jumping from the *Wall Street Journal* to a football game to something about fashion. They were a bunch of demigods, capable of doing a thousand things at once. I hadn't spoken and eaten at the same time in nearly a year. Even at the café, I never ate until Bella and Linda had returned to the kitchen. I could talk slowly, and I could eat slowly—but not at the same time. My family's words and stories kept coming, switching directions. Often, as much as I wanted to join in, my mouth felt like an empty tunnel, filled with the possibility of passage but with no cars passing through. Spoken English, apparently, had become a second language to me. Everything they said I saw in pictures, and the pictures became confusing—it was hard to translate what they were saying into something I could understand.

"So what's the takeaway?" Dirk said to me as we stood at the dessert buffet. The selection was overwhelming: Apple pie. Key lime pie. Boston cream pie. Blueberry pie. Mom's forest torte. Häagen Dazs. Fresh raspberries. Peanut butter cookies. Brussels cookies. Milanos. Brownies. Fresh whipped cream.

"The takeaway?"

"You know. From your life in the woods."

The takeaway. What I saw in my mind was a pizza box—the pizza inside topped with evergreens, a driving snow, mountains in the distance. "I'm sorry?"

He stepped closer. He was a former college football player, solidly built, his venture capital business highly successful. He was accustomed to getting answers to his questions. "Say you're giving a three-minute PowerPoint to the board. To some group that's going to fund solitude projects for other kids. What's the takeaway?"

I tried to picture *power point*, but that didn't help much either. And why would anyone fund kids to do what I was doing? His questions seemed slightly crazy. But this was his house, I was his guest. I wanted to oblige. Besides, I'd always liked Dirk.

His hunger couldn't have been more different from mine, but he was always hungry—for the newest, for the latest, for the best. And now he had sniffed out something in me; he was hard on the trail.

"He wants the *answers*," Susan said, handing Dirk a glass of wine, nudging him playfully.

"Not the answers, exactly. Just the lesson," he said, in a voice suitable for conveying a lesson.

No lessons came to mind. I could hear the football game playing in the room behind us. Someone had just scored a touchdown. Susan suddenly grabbed my arm. "You're like a modern Thoreau. Like that kid from *Into the Wild*. Except you're still living, of course. Important distinction."

I tried to smile. To play along. I was sorry about it, I wanted to be able to say something, but there was no way to give the pictures in my mind—the way the woods looked behind the house, the way the chickadees darted branch to branch, the way the far mountains looked from the vista. "That's better than the Unabomber, I guess."

Susan broke into a desperate smile. "There's the old Howie," she said. "Witty. Fun." She squeezed my arm, as though to dispense more of the old me.

I nodded politely, stepped away, and helped myself to a piece of the apple pie. But I knew what she'd meant. As the words had emerged from my mouth, I'd felt a soft pain by my cheek, a wing-beat, a familiar shadow. And I hadn't entirely minded it.

The second cop stopped me the following morning. Accommodations at my aunt and uncle's house in Newburgh were tight, and under the pretext of giving everyone more room, I camped in the backyard in my tent. I needed to be alone. I needed to breathe. There'd been almost no moments, apart from the conversation with Susan, where I'd felt close to anyone. The headache had fought its way back into my neck, into my eye. Mom pleaded against the backyard. She seemed to fear losing me in the hedge, in the weeping willow. Aunt Betty didn't like the idea either: this was her domain, and never in twenty-five years had anyone slept back there. There were *dangers*—deer, skunks, raccoons. But no one really wanted to argue with me.

The temperature dropped below freezing, but my sleeping bag worked fine, and at daybreak, as always, I rose and went for a walk. The grass was hoary with frost, the street was silent, the morning air bracing. There was the tight, vinegary scent of frozen crab apples, mixed with the scents of the dead leaves. The sky was beginning to lighten. Not a quarter mile away, I came to the Desmond Estate, which had been converted into a campus for a local college. Its broad lawns displayed massive, gnarled trees with black name tags. I ignored the paved paths and drifted across the grass, the sides of my boots darkening with the melting frost. The steel-gray river, which I'd glimpsed from the brow of a hill, was now a single glinting snake in the morning sun. The morning was beautiful. The whole Hudson River Valley was beautiful. I thought of the last page of *The Great Gatsby*, the green land flowering before the Dutch sailors' eyes, that last moment, Fitzgerald wrote, when man was face to face with something commensurate with his capacity for wonder. I thought of Dirk's inadvertent similarity to Gatsby—the unused rooms of his house, the twenty-two televisions, which were maybe the convenient, modern stand-in for glittering parties, and I wondered what part of the past he was trying to recapture. I wondered if it was similar to the feeling of community my parents were trying to recapture every time they drove through Newburgh. And I wondered if it was similar to what I was trying to recapture by living in the woods, just in my own solitary way.

When I came out of the estate, I followed the low stone wall beside the road. A large bird, a hawk of some kind, perched atop a dead tree. The tree had been hit by lightning, the top of it just a blackened shard, a spire towards the sky. Gazing up at the hawk, I heard a car approaching from behind me. I didn't turn. Then a car door groaned open, closed, and there were slow footsteps. *Not again.* I turned to see a police officer, one hand resting on his billy club.

"How we doing this morning?"

"OK."

"We have a problem?"

I realized I wasn't wearing any pants. Just my wool watchman's cap, a heavy sweater, and long underwear bottoms. "No problems, sir."

"We do know that's private property." He gestured with his chin toward the Desmond Estate.

"I won't steal it."

His hand tightened once around his club, released. This was conspicuously not his first day on the job. The composed skepticism of his eyes was alarming, as though the world had been arranged to deceive him. He liked the job, but he didn't like doing it—he didn't like doing it because of people like me.

Just then, a roar spread into the leaves from the far side of the hill, and another police car, blue lights flashing, topped the rise. I thought it might hit me. The siren seemed to scream from inside my face. The car skidded, spraying loose gravel into the stone wall, and a short, broad-shouldered officer emerged. He moved slowly, his hips swaying with his heavy belt.

"Problem here?"

"No, sir."

"What's your business?" He sounded as though he were a secretary for the day. He had a strikingly handsome face, but given his height, it only diminished his authority.

"Just going for a morning walk," I said. "It's very pretty here."

"It's very pretty here." He pulled down his mouth. "He says it's pretty. Identification."

"Sir?"

"Do you have identification? Driver's license? Green card?"

Green card. I thought of the trees. I thought of Gatsby and the green breast of land. "My license is in my tent."

"And where is your *tent?*" the first cop said, the word dirty in his mouth, as though waiting back in this tent would be five filthy children and a woman who looked at me with hatred in her eyes.

"Sir?"

"Your tent. With your ID. Where is it?"

My legs suddenly felt naked. I took a shaky breath and tried to translate myself into terms they might understand. I told them my aunt and uncle lived on Bryant Drive, just up the road. I told them my other uncle lived across town. I told them my parents had grown up here, gone to Newburgh Free Academy. I told them my grandfather had built his own house on North Street. I told them we came to Newburgh every Thanksgiving, and that's why I was here. They didn't seem quite ready to believe me, but as I was finishing, my uncle Don stopped at the stop sign at the end of Bryant Drive in his Isuzu Trooper.

He rolled down his window. "Howie, that you?"

"Everything's fine," I called.

"Are you sure?"

"All set."

"Officers?" The sun winked off the gold chain around his neck. Even at a distance, he looked like a matinee idol from the fifties, surprised by cops who weren't played by fellow actors.

"All set here. Just having a chat."

"He's a little different, my nephew."

The short cop made a snorting sound, and after a moment Don drove off, headed into town. The day waited.

"We had a complaint," the first cop said. "A woman in one of these houses. Called in a suspicious male."

"Suspicious male?"

"Lady said you were walking real slow. Looking at things. She said you kept looking up at the sky. Thought you were probably on drugs. Made her nervous."

"Neighborhood watch," the short cop said. "Sorry about that."

I didn't know what to say. Apparently, danger averted, they didn't know either. I wondered what would have happened if I'd been black, or if my uncle hadn't driven up, or if I'd wised off to them. I thought about the prison just on the other side of the Hudson, the electrified fences I saw out the car window every trip to Newburgh, and the enormous insane asylum on the eastbound side of the highway, and I wondered if I was admitted there, thrown behind those faceless windows, if I would ever manage to get out. It was strange to think my family's history had protected me. Strange to think family wasn't just a series of walls to keep you in one place, for better or for worse, but a way of keeping others out—a way of keeping them from fitting you into whatever narrative seemed closest at hand, whatever stereotype seemed most readily available.

The cops were waiting. I turned and pointed to the dead tree, to show them what I'd been looking at. I didn't expect them to fully understand, I wasn't going to try to explain, but I wanted to bridge the gap somehow, to make an effort at some kind of cross-cultural exchange. There was no rush now. We were outside. The morning was quiet.

They followed my finger. But there was nothing, just a dead tree. The hawk must have taken flight in the commotion. They didn't bother questioning me any further. I was harmless, not worth the time. They walked back to their squad cars, armored themselves in the roar of the engines, and rolled back into the day.

Back in my tent in the backyard, I took my time getting dressed. The sunlight through the tent walls turned my arms and legs blue. Everything, including my thoughts, felt aquatic. Watery mirrors were everywhere. They were in the eyes of my family. In the suspicion of the neighbors. In the disdain of the police. I was a concern, a drifter, a threat. My belt was too tight. My hair was too wild. My beard was too bushy. I didn't fit in, which was exactly how I'd felt before moving to the woods, but now everyone could see it. Maybe it had been better to hide it. Or maybe it had been right to go to the woods, so I didn't have to. *What was so fucking strange about wanting to go for a walk in the morning, wanting to look at the trees? What was so fucking strange about wanting to be fully human?* I was furious. And I was hurt. And I wanted to go home—back to the woods.

9

To drive straight back to the woods, to have no other company stored up for the winter, felt dangerous. I wondered if I could trust myself, wondered how I'd been so wrong. No one, apart from the police officers, had looked deeply into my eyes. No one had even felt at ease in my presence, probably because I'd felt so uneasy myself. There'd been no conversation like the one with Ray, no seeing the chickadee movements behind anyone's words. And what I had seen had only confused me. The extra space around me, my expanded hearing and vision, had only made me more remote from my family rather than bringing me closer to them. If my visit had been a practice run, a preview of what my return from the woods would offer, then there was no reason to return.

From somewhere, hundreds of miles behind me, I heard Andrew. He'd always told me the last place I would feel comfortable was with my family. *That's the finals of Wimbledon*, he'd said after my return from Italy. *You need to start off with warm-up tournaments, with easier competition.* Nearly everything with Andrew was a sports metaphor, and he was nearly always right. I could feel his presence slowly filling the car—a distant caution, a warning not to keep driving. Despite myself, despite my backwoodsman pride, I knew I needed his help.

He'd left the pro tennis tour the previous summer, was living in Cambridge again, getting his master's at Harvard Divinity School. He'd played in the first round of Wimbledon, had some good wins, but mostly he'd been relegated to the satellite and challenger tournaments, playing on broken seashells in Indonesia, or on rolled dung in South Africa, or waiting as a goat crossed his court in India. He'd sent me a few long, mostly philosophical, letters, c/o General Delivery, West Glover, Vermont. He quoted Rumi, Plato, Zen philosophers—anything he could get his hands on to talk about jumping levels, letting go and playing freely under pressure, letting the game move through him. Then, on a piece of sky-blue stationery sent from the Philippines, he'd written this:

Dear Duck,

Wish I could talk to you, just get it all out there, but this will work. Something happened, dude. It was at the tourney here, second round, against this giant from Ukraine. I finally felt it. People talk about playing in the zone, but really, it feels like you're free of any zone. You're just playing. You can do anything, put the ball anywhere. Everything's so slow. It was the beginning of the second set. I hit a return up the line and this thing clicked in. I wasn't thinking about anything. That part of my mind, the governor part, was gone. The governor, that's the part that governs you, that questions everything, that's afraid to lose. It's weird, it's the part I tend to identify as myself, but suddenly he was gone. And it's just me without the governor, which doesn't feel like me. It's more like the way Homer says sing in me Muse, and this tennis muse is playing through you. And you're effortless. I mean, you should have seen me, dude. Drop shots. Half volleys. Everything. But then it hit me—I couldn't make that shot, I'm not supposed to make that shot. And then my muse got nervous, like I didn't really trust her. And then I'm just back in my sneakers, the sun's in my eyes—and I can still hit the ball, but it was over.

By the way, here's a question I've been mulling. Do you think the Buddha could beat Pete Sampras?

Hope you're staying warm,
Andrew

There was nowhere for me to write him back, but that letter kept me feeling like he was my closest friend in the world. He was also searching—searching for something he couldn't quite name.

At the split between 91 North and 84 East, I headed east, which would lead to the Mass. Pike and to Cambridge. Andrew had suggested I stop by on my return north, and though I'd put him off, I needed to take the chance. I needed to know I wasn't an alien everywhere. I needed to feel the possibility some life outside the woods still existed for me. I needed to know the river could still be crossed.

It was night when I came into Boston. The green signs for Framingham and Natick and Weston floated past, the glowing white words familiar and strange, carrying with them an unwritten guidebook about what kind of person lived where, a kind of map of assumptions that no longer seemed true, as they'd been predicated on my being a kid from Brookline, on knowing where I fit in and where I didn't. The eastern sky was vaguely dark, illumined by a jaundiced glow. Then it seemed the stars had fallen from the sky. They were so close. It was impossible to find Orion or the Dipper or the North Star, but somehow the stars grew larger as I drew near. After a slow, wondrous moment, I remembered what I was seeing, remembered *how* I was supposed to see: skyscrapers. Driving towards them was still gorgeous and strange, like approaching a dazzling hall of mirrors, the well-lit pavement leading into their luminous heart as unlikely as the yellow brick road. All of this was built by people, planned by people, used by people: every overpass and support beam and off-ramp, every street sign and streetlight, every office window, every sidewalk, every billboard, every apartment building, every convenience store, fencepost, parking lot, restaurant, truck, license plate—everything, in every direction, a testament to people's ingenuity and industriousness, thousands and thousands of people's handiwork visible in every glance. The city was a temple with an alternate god. The city was a temple to people. The variety of trees and insects and animals, the variety that had emerged in the woods in concert with each other over millions of years, had been replaced by an alternate course in evolution. Everything here had been formed by one species, for one species. The city skyline looked dazzlingly complex, but really it was dazzlingly one-sided. What could be more extreme than living in a city? In comparison, living in the woods seemed conservative, in every sense of the word.

Cars kept passing me on either side. To try to keep my mind quiet and my eyes on the road, I focused on license plate numbers, a habit I'd developed as a boy to stave off boredom. But now I couldn't help noticing the model names above the taillights or on the doors as cars passed. Rabbit, Taurus, Jaguar. Ram, Impala, Cougar. Skylark, Topaz, Denali. Everything was supposedly here: a menagerie of animals from around the world, precious stones, even the Alaskan tundra.

The world is too much with us.

The line floated into my head with the sodium glow of the highway lights. I couldn't remember where it came from. But I knew the next line was something about the getting and spending—something about the pressures that kept us from paying attention to the natural world. It was such a bizarre question, of just where the world was. Maybe it wasn't in the city at all.

Maybe all these animals and all these stars were just hundreds of facsimiles that had been imported, replacements to help us forget the strange bargain we had made.

As I followed down the spiral exit for Cambridge, I remembered reading about pygmies in the Amazon who'd lived their whole lives in the rainforest, immersed in a leafy maze or in small clearings with the sky high above them, and when forced from their habitat, they had no vision for the middle distance. A horse across an open field became an insect; a boat far upstream couldn't possibly be large enough to carry people. They could only see, and could only think, in some overlapping combination of the celestial and the close at hand. They couldn't live in the comfortable middle.

I feared, as I crossed the bridge over the Charles, that my way of seeing had developed a similar gap. When it came to people, maybe I'd lost acuity for the middle ground of daily life. There was just a dull blind spot there—a phantom sense of loss, an echo of something I could no longer perceive.

Andrew's greeting was mercifully understated. He'd prepared a welcome offering, and wanted it to speak for itself. A bottle of Gatorade, toast with peanut butter and honey, a clean white towel for a shower. He seemed to know I needed time to sit still, to let the miles slow down below me, to take in where I was. He lived on the third floor, in a one-bedroom apartment on Cambridge Street, a few blocks from Harvard Square. The moldings and the hardwood floor were the same vintage as Adams House. The blue futon was the same, too. As was the scent of radiator, old books, and dried paint, but there was a trace of something new, maybe incense or the leather sandals, which he said he'd bought in Bombay. On his desk was an assortment of seashells, a harmonica, a photo of himself as a little boy with a tennis racket as big as he was, and the cover of *Leaves of Grass* in a picture frame. Walt Whitman's bearded madman face peered out at the room like a relative.

He sat at his desk as I dressed after the shower. I'd never felt awkward changing in front of him, but now I angled myself away. My body felt too slight, like it didn't belong here, like the room and the city outside were too strong for it.

" '*I came in from the wilderness, a creature void of form, come in she said, I'll give you shelter from the storm.*' Jesus. You listening to any Dylan up there?"

"Not really."

"You should. '*How does it feel? To be on your own, no direction home.*' You know?"

I nodded.

" '*Where have you been, my blue-eyed son?*' "

"You play the harmonica?"

He wheeled his chair over to the desk, picked up the harmonica, put it down. "No, but I want to. I'm going to learn." He wheeled back over to the futon. "You are looking a little angular," he said.

"No food at Thanksgiving."

"Really? Hard times?"

"Matt counted more pies than people."

He smiled. "How is the future senator?"

I said he seemed the same.

"And the rentals?"

"The rentals?"

"You know, the parentals, the parietals, the occipitals."

It took me a long moment. This was how we used to talk. His last name was Rueb, and I'd called him Ruby, Rubicon, the Rubaiyat of Omar Khayyam, sometimes Measles, Mumps, Rubella. There was a terrible movie called *Howard the Duck*, and he'd called me Duck, Duck Soup, Duck Sauce.

"Hemispheric," I said.

"They didn't give you a timeline, did they?"

"For what?"

"You know," he said. "For coming back?"

The possibility hadn't occurred to me, and I didn't understand why it had occurred to him. I stared at him. He wheeled backwards. A seashell clattered to the floor. He leaned over, picked it up, held it in his hand. "I'm just surprised they didn't say something."

"My grandmother's eighty-fifth is in March. They want me to go to a party in Florida. That's all they said."

"Put on your party hat."

I said nothing.

"That grandmother shit is serious, dude. You know how your mom gets."

I asked him about the picture of Walt Whitman.

To my relief, he began talking about the books he read on tour, and about leaving the tour, and about his classes at the Div. School. The highway and the strangeness of the city were still vibrating below me. Sitting there on the blue futon felt similar to being at college, but it didn't feel similar. It felt more like I was eavesdropping on the conversation, like I couldn't afford the comfort of being there.

I slept on the futon but didn't sleep well. Lights kept banking on the ceiling, opening shifting panels of light and closing them, like multiple moons orbiting the room. A car alarm shrieked outside like a demented bird. Upstairs, someone dropped something heavy. There wasn't darkness. There wasn't quiet. I wondered how Andrew managed to sleep. I wondered how anyone managed to sleep. I wondered what it meant that my fears were the opposite of a child's. It was night, and I was afraid of the light, afraid of the noise.

———

That next morning was the hardest. We followed the brick side-walks into Harvard Square. A few yellow maple leaves lingered on the boughs. It was football weather, the kind of morning I'd loved as a student: girls in sweaters, the air crisp but the sun warm in pockets, everything sharp, everything possible. An-drew had studying to catch up on in Lamont. It was my idea to walk into the Square with him—to use him as a kind of protec-tive escort, a human shield.

The largest city I'd visited in Vermont was Newport. It had one main drag, with four or five traffic lights, a Wendy's, a su-permarket, and a movie theater with two screens. I'd gone to the movies once, late during the previous winter, just to see people, even if they were only made of light. They were showing a se-quel that looked very loud and a movie called *Castaway. At the edge of the world*, the poster said, *his journey begins.* Not much promise of conversation, but it seemed a possible clue, a mirror I might safely confront. It was afternoon, only three people in the darkened theater. Tom Hanks's character seemed familiar to me and yet very unfamiliar—his solitude on the island was so vocal, so visual, so outward. I wondered if I was strange not to have befriended inanimate objects, not to have pleaded with a volleyball, or, in my case, with the woodstove or the shovel. What was even stranger was how fluent he was. He hadn't lost language at all. And his return, the scene with the woman who had been his fiancée, didn't seem realistic either. He was too at ease. When she touched him on the arm in her kitchen, the touch shot up my own arm, and I didn't understand how he didn't melt into her, or push her away—something. I walked out of the theater into the early winter dusk, purple clouds above the brightly lit sign of the Wendy's, and I felt even lonelier than when I'd gone in, because my loneliness hadn't been on the screen.

But I was with Andrew now, it was a quiet Sunday morning, and the day breathed promise. I was ready to see Harvard Square, to see faces, maybe even more faces than I'd seen in the past year. As we passed Ellery Street, a young woman in shorts and sweatshirt popped out onto her front steps, an eager black lab beside her, tail slapping against her leg. She said good morning. Then she headed off on a jog, the dog trotting alongside, her blonde ponytail swinging back and forth, a happy metronome.

"Just taking a rest, buddy?"

Without knowing why, I'd sat down on the sidewalk. Her skin in the sunlight, the open friendliness of her face. It was something in her ease, her vitality. Even the dog had seemed beautiful. I looked up at Andrew. "Did you see her?"

"Yes."

My instinct had been to absorb the feeling, as though I'd just seen a deer bounding with impossible grace through knee-high snow. But she wasn't a deer. *She was what I was.*

"Everything OK there?"

I made myself stand up. "You saw her?"

"Pretty sure."

"She was *very* attractive," I said.

"Wasn't bad."

Andrew glanced at me, then started walking again at the same speed, which seemed very fast. I struggled to keep up, but this was my morning walk, and maybe from practice my eyes felt almost as slow as they did in the woods. Everything was entering me deeply again. I looked over at Andrew. It struck me how healthy he was, how vital. The glossiness of his dark hair, the stubble on his jaw. He moved effortlessly. He cut through the air more easily than I did, like he was more aerodynamic. As with the jogger, I could see the wonder of his existence.

"How you doing, Duck?"

"There's so much beauty," I said.

He coughed. "You sound a little like Uncle Walt. Miracles everywhere. You read *Leaves of Grass?*"

"No."

"You should, dude. Absolutely."

I nodded, noticing another woman on the opposite side of the street. She had short black hair, a bright turquoise scarf around her neck. She walked as though pushing through on-coming waves—so solid, so purposeful, so alive.

"Then again, maybe not. We've got to get you back in training. Back up to speed. You've been in the Sahara."

"The Sahara?"

"The desert, dude. The metaphorical desert. You've got to pace yourself. Can't drink too much at one time. We run into a really hot girl, she's liable to strike you dead."

I saw the jogger again in my mind. She was naked, her breasts and golden hair like so much sunlight washing over me. It didn't seem the worst way to go.

I kept falling behind. Even when I caught up, Andrew stayed a step or two ahead, as though his shoulder were my companion. Had he grown even more athletic on the tennis tour, or was I just terribly out of shape? I wondered if maybe I should shave my beard. And then a painful thought popped into my head. I wondered if Andrew was embarrassed to be seen with me.

Suddenly, there was a dull roar, an engulfing vibration. There had been no breeze, no warning, nothing but the smell of the sunlight, the brick sidewalk, the leaves. But the bus—it was a city bus racing down Mass. Ave.—swallowed everything, its wake of wind covering the street like an ocean wave.

Andrew didn't notice. I tried to relax, to breathe slowly. I remembered the cool under the brick archway entrance to the Yard. I remembered how I'd always liked that feeling, a kind of ritual bath every morning before moving into the realm of learning. But as we approached the archway, a high-pitched screeching pierced the air behind us. It sounded like a carousel being put through a shredder—so many painted metal ponies grinding under the blades. My fingers in my ears, I turned in horror. There was just a white Cambridge cab, a green shamrock on its door, pulling over by Bartley's Burgers. The door opened and a well-dressed woman got out. She thanked the driver. No pedestrian rushed to check under the hood. No painted ponies were extracted from beneath the tires. The cab eased back into the flow of traffic.

"You all right, Duck?"

Embarrassed, I pulled my fingers from my ears.

"The brakes a little loud for you?"

I looked down Mass. Ave. towards Central Square, angry, assaulted, scouting for more cabs, more buses, more possible offenders.

"You've probably got to adjust your equalizer a little bit."

The air around me still felt blurry. "My what?"

"Your equalizer. You know—how much beauty you see, how much bus. Maybe you've got to filter some things out."

I didn't know why he was talking to me here. I just wanted to get inside the cool brick archway, away from the street.

"You know, maybe you could be a little less sensitive. Maybe there's some middle ground." He was nodding as he spoke, as though being very patient with a child.

"Is that what Uncle Walt says? The Middle Ground? Is that one of his poems?"

We stood in front of the archway. My tone was not nice. Andrew knew exactly what I was saying.

"Listen, I'm just—"

"Maybe I'm not like you. Back from your adventures with a pair of leather sandals from India. Back with some seashells on your desk."

He crossed his arms, looked down at his feet. He absorbed the blow. Everything around us was on his side and he knew it. "Your call, dude."

We passed silently through the shadow under the archway, and stopped as we came into the quadrangle of Tercentenary Theater, the paths criss-crossing under the oaks. Our graduation ceremony had been held here just five years earlier. Crimson banners riffling in the June sunlight, rows and rows of proud parents arrayed beneath the massive columns of Widener Library. The quad was nearly empty now. Andrew shifted his backpack on his shoulder. He was getting his study-face ready, preparing to go face his competition. He'd wanted to help me, but the quarters were getting too close, and maybe a little too strange. He had his own life to worry about, his own changes. He glanced at his watch. No one said anything. I hated feeling needy, especially as I didn't know what I needed. Only three years earlier, on a hike in northern New Hampshire, Andrew had grabbed my hand. He'd asked a few nervous questions about bears before we started, and half a mile up the trail, there was a crackling boom behind us, a great rustling of leaves. A hand was suddenly holding mine, Andrew's face utterly still. I said it was a large tree branch falling—not a bear, a bear wouldn't make that much noise. Slowly, Andrew had loosened his grip.

He shifted his backpack again, looked down at his feet. I was the one afraid now of noises, the one overwhelmed by his surroundings. The one who might have reached for his best friend's hand.

"What happened to miracles everywhere?" I said. "What happened to letting go of the governor?"

"Listen, you want to be able walk down the street like a normal human being, or don't you?"

The answer was supposed to be obvious. But I didn't want to haze my eyes, my ears. Not after everything I'd been through to learn how to see again. If I tried to turn down my senses to allow for the taxis and the buses, for all the images that didn't make sense, wouldn't I lose the chickadees, too? Wouldn't I lose everything—the ability to know where I was and who I was? Besides, I didn't know if I could do it anymore, even if I wanted to, if there was any way to reverse course.

As we came alongside the front of Widener, its massive columns more imposing and more meaningless than ever, I could feel Andrew looking at me. He was still waiting for my answer. Senior year, when a sound had startled me, I would recover far more quickly. He would go on talking, I would listen gratefully, and our conversation would pull away from my discomfort. But our old patterns weren't enough now. I was worse off than both of us had thought.

"Tell me," he said, "don't you want to be comfortable here? Don't you want to be able to come back?"

I didn't know how to explain. I didn't know where to start. "I don't know," I said. "Maybe not."

10

Winter wasn't shy. It didn't care that I'd been away. Before my trip, the snow had just been learning the shape of things—lining the black branches of the apple trees in the meadow, tracing the circular grain on top of the fenceposts, as though uncovering map after map of some distant world. But now the snow knew where to fall. It wasn't overzealous, but it kept coming. And I didn't resist the seduction, the welcome home.

My snowshoeing jaunts grew longer, the trails less and less clear through the trees, less and less necessary. There was so much to explore: the heavier feel of the cold in the shadows of the pine and spruce, the thin, ice-cold brooks rimmed with ice, the hidden copses of silver birch, their enclaves turning enchanted in the afternoon sun. I crossed fences that had been dwarfed by the snowfall, their barbed wire reduced to hieroglyphics peeking above the ground. I took off my snowshoes and forded creeks. All of it felt like home—not so much my land as land I belonged to, land where nothing could go wrong. And when something did, as when I came upon a house a few miles to the west and saw what appeared to be a human body hanging from the front porch, then hurried closer to find it was a black bear hanging from a noose, I ignored it, turned around, and snowshoed home. Omens did not interest me. At least not omens that came from other people. Hunters, distant neighbors, the headlines at the C&C—it was all the same. Communication that didn't come from the sky, or the snow, or the bears themselves had nothing to do with me.

My daily rituals remained the same. Tending the fire in the woodstove, making mint tea, taking long walks. The constant effort at opening the eyes of my eyes, the ears of my ears. Linda posted a sign in the café window politely informing her patrons the café would be closed until May due to heating costs. My trips to the C&C became less frequent, usually with no words spoken. But I did feel a new need to establish my own voice among the woods—or not really my own voice but a voice that would allow the silence around me to take form. This way I might play a role, the way everything in the woods played a role; I would become part of the ecosystem, even if it wasn't exactly clear what my poems were feeding. And, perhaps, I could eventually turn them into a book, could use the money I earned to keep living here, to make this way of living into my way of life.

It seemed a solid plan. The poems came to me as I shoveled the roof at night, or as I carried logs in for the woodstove, or as I washed my hands at the sink. I'd play with the words in my mind, count the syllables, try different ways of breaking the lines. After my walk the next morning, I'd mount the steep stairs to the bedroom, then go up the extra two stairs to the desk, and write the poems on individual pieces of blank white paper, my hand long and loose. Every morning there was another one or two to transcribe from the day before.

As the snow bowed the wooden railing outside the window, and the drifts deepened on the deck like waves washing up onto a ship, there were fewer and fewer words on the page, as though my voice itself was beginning to vanish under the snow. Sometimes the words felt like footprints, harder and harder to find. But the stack grew beside me on the desk, proof of my existence, of time passing. And maybe the blank lines and the growing quiet of the poems were a sign of progress. After all, I wasn't searching for my own reflection or my own personal voice but for the voice that would remain when my own reflection ceased to be.

Nat's son was showing up to plow more than necessary. Even when there were only five or six new inches, snow I easily could have driven through, his father's truck emerged out of the trees at the far end of the field. In the fall, Nat Jr. had delivered wood—a heap left by the garage, like a giant's matchsticks spilled from a box—and I'd seen him driving out. Yes, he said, his dad was in the hospital but nothing to be worried about, the old man had more fight than a chainsaw. After the first major nor'easter, Nat Jr. didn't come for a week, but now every time the snow fell he appeared like part of the weather. He never stopped to talk. Sometimes he raised one finger from the wheel, the way his father had.

Which is how, one slate-gray afternoon, I realized it. His coming wasn't a good sign. There could be only one explanation for why he made the half-hour drive from Newport when there wasn't any need. It was a way of doing something for his father, even if his father never knew. It was a way of caring for him. The frequent intrusion began to annoy me, and I figured with Nat's recovery the visits would taper off. But as January slipped into February, nothing changed, and I knew part of my annoyance at Nat Jr. was really my annoyance with myself, with my own inaction. I'd done nothing for Nat, nothing to see how he was. I became determined to talk to his son, to ask for an update, but he never stopped the truck, not even when I signaled him. Maybe the music inside the cab was too loud. Or maybe he knew what I would ask, and he didn't want to answer.

That night, I imagined driving to the hospital, lying to the nurse, saying I was family. There had to be a way to see him. *And then what? I'd sit by his bedside, hold his hand, tell him how much his snowplowing meant to me?* Something about my need for Nat didn't make sense. We barely knew each other. The desire to see him, I thought, was a weakness. I wouldn't be going to the hospital for him, I'd be going for me—for some kind of emotional handhold, even if Nat didn't say a word. In my mind, I saw a well, tiny branches sticking out from the icy wall, and instead of just letting myself fall, instead of trusting that I could survive whatever was at the bottom, I was grasping for something midway down. I didn't want that need. I didn't want any personal connection holding me up. That branch would just strain and snap under real weight. I needed to let go and trust in the bottom of the well. Only once I touched bottom, felt my feet and hands on something solid, something beyond which there was nothing else, would I know what to trust—and how to begin again.

A few afternoons later, the phone rang. I thought it might be the hospital, even though no one there had my number, or maybe it was Nat Jr.—so I picked up. It was Mom. Her voice was so loud but so far away. She said they'd found a direct flight from Burlington to Fort Lauderdale for me. Everyone was going to be at Nanny's party, even Susan and Dirk, who would be flying back from Italy. The snow was falling in large, desultory flakes, a kind of afterimage of the storm from the night before. I'd just come back in from shoveling the roof, was still in my snowpants. I sat down in my phone position. "I can't do it," I said.

"You need an afternoon flight? There is an afternoon flight. Hold on, let me get Dad on the line, too."

I waited. The woods seemed to go on for hundreds and hundreds of miles.

"Howie, you there? So I've got the flight times here."

"I'm sorry. I can't make that trip."

The line fell silent. "What do you mean you can't make *that trip?*"

"It's your grandmother's eighty-fifth birthday," Mom said. "Everyone is coming. The whole family is coming. We talked about this. Susan and Dirk are coming back from Italy, for God's sake. We'll pay for the flight. We're more than happy to pay."

I said nothing.

"We understand spending time with the family might be hard for you," Dad said, his voice calm again, lawyerly. "Sometimes it's hard for me or your mother to take time, but sometimes you have to subordinate your own interests. That's what being part of a family means."

"I tried at Thanksgiving."

"You do understand occasionally making a sacrifice for someone else. Don't you care enough about your mother and your family to do that? To sacrifice a few days?"

I pictured myself as an effigy, burning on a chaise lounge by the pool.

"I don't understand," Mom said, less to me than to whoever had captured her son. "I don't understand how this is possible."

"I wish I could explain."

"Carl, hang up the phone," she said.

"Are you sure?"

"Hang up!" There was a cough, a scuffling noise, and then the line was clear. "I will not promise you a second chance," she said. "Do you understand me?" I could see her, on the phone in the kitchen, glaring at me as though I'd become a perfect stranger, her eyes a one-way trip past all the years I'd been her son, past whatever she had believed she knew of me.

"This doesn't have to do with you, Mom."

"Of course it has to do with me!"

After she hung up, the snow kept falling. It had been falling for days. The light on the floorboards below the windows was gray, dense with silence. The room was an emptiness and fullness at the same time. There was a thickness in the air, a density that filled the room, that filled all of me, right up to my teeth. As though the house were showing me a glimpse of my remains.

The truck's sound shouldered into the gathering dusk. I'd been walking alongside the open field, watching the pockets of blue in the snow, trying to catch the moment as they dissolved into black. Beyond the field, streaks of purple rode stowaway in the keels of the clouds.

Nat Jr. slowed to a halt alongside me, the snow creaking under the tires, and he rolled down the window. The engine ran, but no music played from the radio. He was holding a cigarette. He looked up at me after he lit it. "Thought you'd want to know," he said.

I couldn't catch up to the words, to their meaning. They seemed to run out ahead of me into the field.

"Passed a few nights ago." He took a deep drag on his cigarette, then glared down at it, as though its taste was disappointing.

"I'm so sorry."

"Life's a bitch and then you die, right?" The blond hair at his collar trembled with the vibration of the truck. His eyelids looked pink, slightly swollen.

"I should have seen him in the hospital."

He exhaled a long plume of smoke. He stared at the glowing lights of dashboard, one hand still on the wheel, as though for indication of what had gone wrong. "Well, I guess that little crush of yours was mutual. He talked about you whenever he came down here. Mom said it was like you was some version of himself he never got to be."

I was stunned. I didn't feel like a version of anything.

"Your father was a good man," I said.

"What would you know about it?"

I didn't want to take my hand off the truck door. It was the closest, I realized, I would ever come to touching Nat again. "I appreciate your coming down here."

"Nothing else to do."

"When's the funeral?"

"All taken care of."

"You mean the arrangements?"

"All taken care of," he said. He leaned towards me, rolled the window back up. Then he raised one finger in parting, threw the truck into reverse, backed at alarming speed into the field, and drove off towards town.

The blue had fled from the field. It seemed I could hear the truck for a long time through the trees. I had the urge to whisper to Nat Jr. that he was jealous of a ghost, of a product of his father's imagination. The truth was I was jealous of that ghost, too—the eager young man who'd stacked wood that first fall, the real backwoodsman, his search underway.

The border of pines at the far end of the field was a silhouette of spires. I wondered what Nat would say if I walked towards it now, that dark church—whether, now that he was gone, he would understand.

The firelight played through the grates. I tried the visualization game, but no clear pictures were coming—there was too much static. The only thing I could focus on was the fire. I could make my vision alternate, back and forth, first seeing it as throwing light into the room, then seeing it as drawing light from the room. The first way, the room grew lighter, the orange glow fanning across the floorboards from the wood burning in the stove; the second way, the room grew darker, the fire feeding on the last bits of light hidden under the table, the last bits of light hidden inside of me. It wasn't a new game, but it made me uneasy now. It was just a seesaw of vision, of mind, but I could feel the question at its fulcrum. *How much more light could I absorb from the woods before the woods absorbed all the light from me?*

I didn't want to go upstairs to bed, didn't trust my mind to be quiet. I needed to talk to someone. Not to Andrew. Definitely not to my parents. It took me awhile, but then I thought of Ray. Not to say anything necessarily, but just to make the room a little more solid with his voice.

I sat down on the daybed and dialed his number. I saw the Hudson River and the New York City night out his window. He picked up on the third ring.

"Howie, I've been thinking about you."

The possibility astounded me. "You were?"

"It's late for you, isn't it?"

"I think so."

"We've got an exam tomorrow, so my mind keeps jumping to more desirable duties."

Maybe it had been a mistake to call.

"You study this stuff long enough, it starts to induce some of the symptoms. Anyway, I needed to call you. I have a story. I've only got ten minutes, but I'll try to be quick."

"Please," I said. "Go ahead."

He described a woman he'd met at a party, how he'd eventually asked her out, and how the previous weekend they'd gone out for coffee. His preamble was a comfort. I didn't care where the story was going. It was a relief to listen to his voice, to hear about a life that was drawn inside clear lines, a life that made sense to its owner. "So we're at this café on the Upper West Side, things are going well, and I notice an attractive woman walk in the door. She's with a man, and they're seated at the table next to us. They're speaking German. She looks familiar, but I'm paying attention to my date, and it's not until I get up to use the bathroom that it hits me."

"What?"

"Milena," he said. "It was Milena."

The firelight wavered and shimmered on the floorboards. It took a few seconds for me to find my voice. "Are you sure?"

"I'm sure. I remembered her from that night at the deli."

It was strange—I'd almost forgotten that they'd met. "Did she say anything to you?"

"So I come back from the bathroom, and her date isn't there, and I think to say something. But before I can, he comes back and sits down."

"You didn't talk to her?"

"She looked at me as we left, really looked at me, but we didn't speak."

"Jesus, Ray."

"But listen. I'm walking with Deb, my date, outside, and she says to me, 'The strangest thing happened while you were in the bathroom. That woman at the table beside us, as soon as her date went to the bathroom, she started telling me all these things. She told me they were married, and she's pregnant, and they live on the Upper West Side. And then she said something really strange. She said they were happy, but there are always parts of your past you wonder about.' Deb said it was like this woman was giving her a message, like she was trying to get it all out before her husband returned."

I was picturing the café, the cups and saucers on the table, picturing Milena urgently saying all this to a woman she did not know.

"It was for you. I'm almost sure. Maybe she promised her husband she'd never be in touch with you again, and this was just her way."

"Maybe."

"Are you OK? You sound kind of strange."

"Was he short?"

"Who?"

"The husband. Was he shorter than her when they came in?"

"I think so. Why? That was the guy from Vienna?"

I needed to get off the phone. I could feel the firelight pulling on me, and I didn't want Ray to hear it. Milena had made a life, a life not without regrets, but with a child on the way, with a future. For her, for what she needed, she had been right. She had made the right decision. And I wondered, for what I needed, if I had been right, too. I wondered why I'd made the choices I'd made. I wondered why my choices didn't seem to lead to any future. I wondered if this house, and these woods, were the only place I could have come.

After a brief reprieve, the snow had begun falling again—falling in the long windows to the woods, falling above my bed and above my desk, and it seemed I was falling with it. My body was falling and filling with the drifting snow, filling and falling with the changing wind. There was no bottom to the falling, no rock bottom where my feet became solid beneath me, but that didn't matter because the falling was everything. There were only the icicles hanging from the eaves, the night dazzle of the falling snow, the curled corpse of a mouse one morning in the mudroom. Reality, it seemed, had entered my bones. I suffered no visions. No voices. The day itself had become the vision and the voice. There was no further surface to peel away, no more scrim to mistrust, nothing larger to belong to. I had never breathed with so much size—never felt so vast and so tiny at the same time, as though my body had become an open doorway without a house, a doorway that was just a means of awareness for everything passing through it. I no longer spoke. No longer thought, other than in a kind of humming. Images drifted through me the way the reflections of migrating birds drift across a pond—

just geometry, a part of the weather. The past and the future no longer occurred. There was only an ever-expanding present. It seemed the day was making itself aware of itself through me. That was all.

The only disturbance, which came especially late in the afternoons, was a recurring migraine, like the one that had surfaced on my drive to Newburgh. It pushed from behind my eye, pushed like a hand reaching for me from out of my past. Ever since the accident, I'd regarded migraines as warnings, as my body's helpful indicator that I was drifting into danger. Too much anxiety, too much confidence, too much anything—a migraine waved its black flag. But now the thunder behind my eye just seemed a final test, some last vestige of myself I had to transcend, even on the days it forced me to crawl out into the snow, overtaken by nausea.

Which is what brought me to the field that night. The pain had wired shut my jaw, made it difficult to eat. The back of my neck had become two taut steel cords, my right shoulder blade rigid through the back of my skull and into my eye. It was dusk, the sky deepening above the trees. I just needed to walk, to keep walking until my eye didn't feel so thick, until it stopped pulsing, until the sharp air granted some relief. But the walking was only spreading the pain. It was my whole body now. I veered off the road into the field. The vomit came on its own, a thin trickle of bile and tea. Tears sprang to my eyes. The heaving kept going, even though there was nothing left. It made me want to surrender, to apologize for things I couldn't explain—to break open whatever buried rooms I'd forgotten. The cold came hot on my face. Eventually I washed my mouth out with snow, rolled onto my back. I could see the North Star, the bow and belt of Orion. The snow was solid under my back. I could feel the cold seeping into my skin, seeping through my snowpants. It was the large hand of the earth resting on my back, holding me as I continued to fall, as the stars appeared overhead. The whole sky seemed the opening of a vast well, and I was down below, looking up at everything. The bottom of the well was cold, so cold, but it was also warm, also burning, and I lay there until I couldn't tell what it was and my eyes closed.

Then I was dreaming. I was in the back stairwell of Roxbury Latin, the stairs abandoned, everyone in class. My mind wasn't entirely clear, but I knew I had killed someone. I couldn't remember my victim or my motive or any of the details. But as I climbed the stairs, my only concern was that the body stay hidden. The door to the Latin classroom was ajar, and my classmates, now in their midtwenties, were translating lines from *The Aeneid.* Their faces were the same as when we were young. I'd stashed the body, I was fairly sure, in the small office on the far side of the classroom. Mr. Brennan took no notice of me. I passed behind his desk, and my classmates took no notice either. I turned the knob on the office door. The low ceiling slanted over me. I closed the door to the classroom. There were three metal lockers. The Latin murmured through the wall. Slowly, I opened the locker on the right. Leaves blew out at me, then wisps of snow. The air inside was dark and cold. Whatever lurked inside was farther back, and just as I caught a glimpse of my corpse, my face frozen white, my eyes open forever, I woke up.

The field was silent. Nothing moved on the snow. The dream swept by me in its entirety, in one long stream. The feeling was all around me, a part of the night, and I could feel myself trying to retreat from it, like from the wreckage of some grisly accident I should never have seen. *Was that what I was doing living this way—killing myself and trying to hide the body?*

My stomach seized. The sky was black. It was hard to move my fingers, my toes. My legs belonged more to the field than to me. My face felt as though the cold had stamped it there, as punishment, as reminder: *you are human*. Slowly, slowly, I assembled myself into an upright creature. Streaks of pain ran like lightning through my feet. I wondered if I should try crawling. But it would take too long. I trudged. I was carrying my own body, struggling under its weight. The black trees lined the dim road, indifferent. If I fell and could not go on, nothing would change. Not the temperature, not the direction of the wind. Not the stars and their movements in the sky. The snow would drift easily around me. A crow's harsh call would greet the morning just the same. I'd be no different than a fallen branch, a fallen fencepost. Small icicles might curl from my nostrils. My death would mean nothing here. I meant nothing here—except to myself. The thought horrified me, urged me forward. It felt like a betrayal. The woods did not care. My throat filled with the thick silence of terror, with the knowledge that no one would hear me if I screamed.

Finally, there was the house, the smell of woodsmoke from the chimney. I trudged past the wood in the garage, past the mudroom, and I was beginning to cry. I didn't know how I would take off my boots without my feet coming off with them. I went to the woodstove, the snow puddling on the floor. My face and hands were burning with the thaw, cracking like plaster casts, like the bottom layer of a mask no human could afford to lose. *I did not want to lose my body*. My hands were bone white, terrifyingly white, but they worked as blunt objects, and in the bathroom I set the shower to warm. The shaking was bad. I couldn't take off my jacket, my snowpants. I ran my hands under lukewarm water at the sink, and when they moved, they ignored all zippers and pulled my jacket over my head like a straitjacket, and pushed off my socks, which were frozen solid inside my boots, my toes marble white, so white, just like my fingers.

In the shower, I was afraid of falling. The water was thousands of tiny arrows piercing my skin. I knelt down on all fours, the water streaming down my back, down my haunches. My body rattled violently. Mom and Dad's faces appeared in front of me in the pebbled water. Their eyes were soft, luminous. I looked at them more deeply than I ever had in real life. I told my mom I loved her. I told my dad I loved him. I apologized to them for everything I had put them through. They looked back at me, looked right back in my eyes, and I had the unmistakable feeling of being seen, of being visible. I had the feeling of being forgiven. *They did not need to know what had driven me here, they only wanted me back.* And not the golden boy version of me or the shamed prodigal son, not some version they even particularly understood. Their love was simply a matter of faith. They loved me with the same love I'd found in the woods, a love below all surfaces—it just wasn't anything they could express, just as it wasn't anything I could express. But I knew, had always known, it was inside them, too.

The water drummed around me, the hard floor dug into my knees. There was no other bottom of the well. There was no other rock bottom. I needed to feel myself against surfaces, to find the shape of what was inside me against something outside me. I needed people, I needed love. I'd wanted to see through all surfaces and to see through myself, but I wasn't a transparent thing. I was bone, sinew, skin. If I lost depth perception when it came to life, if I removed every line so there was no difference between near and far, I'd never survive—maybe as a ghost or as a cipher but not as a human being.

The shaking slowed down, and I felt impossibly lighter, fatigued, almost nothing but bones. I stood up in the shower, made the water hotter. Feeling was coming back in my feet, in my hands. My blood was running like it hadn't for a long time. The vulnerability, the openness, was almost voluptuous. I'd always assumed returning would only be possible under two circumstances—the first was that I no longer needed human love at all, all the love I needed carried inside of me, and the second was that I'd failed miserably and had to return as some broken-down version of the boy I'd been. But there was a third way—to return simply as what I was: a twenty-seven-year-old man, flawed, limited, who was ready to wrestle with his instinct for love, with how horribly vulnerable it would make him. Knowing that no orientation in the world, for anyone, could ever be permanent. Knowing that how I saw would always be changing, depending on who I loved and what I feared.

Later, after I'd dressed in my warmest clothes, I carried the wool blanket from the bed downstairs and lay down in front of the fire. By morning, it had burned down to embers, just a few glowing coals hidden under ash. But I was still there. With the morning light on the floorboards, the snow falling outside. And I felt something I hadn't felt for a long time. A desire for the future. A feeling that good days might be ahead, days with other people, days to look forward to. Days I might allow myself to trust.

I I

It was a few weeks later that the knock came at the door. Each rap sounded alarmingly inside the house, hardening the posts and beams into place with me inside them. I felt sharp flashes, as though I was underwater and something was bobbing on the surface far above me. The blue candle guttered on the table. In the darkened windows to the woods, the reflection of my dinner flickered soft and shadowy, more the idea of a dinner than anything solid. And my image flickered just the same.

In the weeks since my night in the field, I'd understood I was going to leave. I'd told Lev over the phone. I'd told my parents. I didn't know what I would do in Boston, how I would manage—not in the larger sense of the word, not even day to day. I couldn't picture my life there, but I knew I needed to try, knew I needed to start bringing furniture back into the empty room of my life. I understood the months and years ahead would be difficult, but I had no idea just how difficult. I didn't know then that the first doctor I saw in Boston would tell me I weighed 120 pounds, not the 155 pounds I'd written on the form. I didn't know the physical therapist he sent me to would inform me I had the musculature of an eighty-year-old. I didn't know how difficult it would be to get strong again, to resume occupancy in my body. I didn't know that the city, as technology boomed, would only become louder. I didn't know that there would be a terrorist attack on American soil that September, that televisions would appear in almost every restaurant and bar, that there would a constant buzz of information and anxiety. I didn't know that for almost two years straight I'd need to wear earplugs on the street and that with them in my ears I wouldn't see as sharply—the whole day unpleasantly muted, as though I was wearing sunglasses. I didn't know that the sidewalk itself would change. Before going to the woods, I'd overheard an occasional businessman as he stepped out of a taxi, or a stylish young woman broadcasting romantic outrage in front of Au Bon Pain, but in 2001 cell phones were suddenly everywhere, as though another stage of evolution had set in: one hand held to the ear was how humans walked. I didn't know how frightened it would make me—person after person talking into their hands, somewhere else, blind to the day around them. I didn't know I'd feel like Rip Van Winkle, asleep for twenty years, returned to what was functionally a ghost town: a coffee shop full of people, but only the sound of insects in the walls, which weren't insects but fingers typing, typing, burrowing away at the dimensions of time and space, at the human need for being here and now. I didn't know everyone would suddenly have so much to say. I didn't know everyone would suddenly have so little time to listen. I didn't know that just at the time I had learned to slow down, the world would learn to speed up.

And I didn't know that with Andrew's help, I'd learn about a professional tennis player, a Harvard golden boy himself, who had broken his neck and was now making a comeback. I didn't know that in order to talk with him, I'd decide to write an article, and that in doing the interviews, I'd find that being able to listen, to picture what people were saying, really did have a place in modern life, that there was something I could offer: in the right context, people yearned to be heard and to be seen. And I didn't know that the confidence the article would give me would help me on my way to grad school, and even to having a girlfriend again—a reticent, deeply insightful poet from Missouri. And I didn't know that after the article came out, an editor would contact me about writing a book, wondering if there were any human interest stories I might know of and want to tell. A conversation that would lead me to consider my own story—my eye accident, my years in the woods, and my long, strange search to get the world, and my place in it, back into perspective.

The three raps came again. It was probably an emergency, someone was probably in need. Smoke was rising from my chimney. Candlelight spilled out onto the snow. There really wasn't much of a choice. I stepped into my moccasins, crossed the plywood mudroom floor, and opened the door.

A woman stood on the frozen doormat—probably in her midforties, bundled in a long green parka, cheeks faintly red from the cold. In one mittened hand she held a clipboard. "Sorry to disturb you," she said, her breath smoking in the doorway. "Just a few questions. Two thousand senses."

I was confused. I glanced at the form on her clipboard, the number and word in large blocky print. *2000 Census.*

"It won't take long," she said. "Missed a few folks last year. Just trying to get the numbers right."

I asked her in, not sure whether to be relieved or annoyed.

She followed me through the mudroom, and, leaving on her parka, she angled a chair from the table towards the woodstove. Trying to regain my composure, I offered her a cup of tea. She shook her head with the same tight rhythm as her knocking. Apparently, the house's minimalist décor made her more nervous than the darkened roads outside.

"Just a few questions," she said. "You live alone here?"

The answer seemed obvious enough.

"And you have no kids here?"

I only looked at her.

"I do have to ask."

The woodstove was throwing a great deal of heat. I felt too skinny in my t-shirt, all collarbone and ribs. "No kids."

"Name?"

I told her the house's owner was Lev Weissman.

"The form only asks about you. Your information." She unzipped her parka, revealing a sweatshirt underneath, and let out a discreet sigh. Against the dark gray, her eyes became deeper blue.

"Problem?" she said.

I was probably staring like a child. Nothing seemed particularly noteworthy about her, but her details were human details—the pudginess of her fingers at the clipboard's edge, the fading, mottled red in her cheeks.

"Sorry," I said.

"The Census only needs your name. Your birthdate. Your basic information."

Maybe I was the last stop of her night. Maybe someone was waiting for her at home. I imagined the television light flickering in the curtains of a well-kept house, her husband on the couch, soup simmering on the stove. It struck me as a wonder—as something impressive and mysterious. There was some life that she came from.

"Your name?" she said.

The whole house seemed to be listening. A log popped and shifted in the woodstove. The sound of my name in my head felt strange to me. But she was waiting, pencil poised. And the quiet felt different now, like there was an opening in it.

So I spoke my own name. The shapes rusty in my mouth. It almost hurt, like running into an old friend on the street, someone who makes you slightly uneasy because he remembers more about you than you do about him.

"Could you spell it?"

"Yes."

"Would you?"

And I did.

It was a clear May morning, the field still ankle-deep with mud. As the car rode the ruts, the puddles plashing under the tires, I felt myself saying good-bye to everything—to the apple trees in the meadow, to the trail into the woods, to the chickadees, to the field and all the nights and mornings I'd walked beside it, to the very smell of the air. It was childish, but something in me felt like a child, or, really, like a young man setting out from home for the first time. I didn't know what lay ahead of me, but I felt prepared. There was solid ground inside me now—not answers to any specific questions, but a physical understanding that I needed surfaces, however false, however temporary, to get down to the truth beneath them, an understanding that while I wasn't only who I was to other people, without other people it would be nearly impossible to get down to what else I might be. These woods had given me a second chance, a way to learn to see again, and now I was leaving their embrace, like an animal shoved by its mother out of the den. But I was also the mother aware that it was weaning time, aware that if the young didn't leave now, he might never leave and might never have the chance again.

I passed Nat's trailer and said a silent prayer for him, passed the cows on the hillside and the outbuildings of the Mooreland farm, and felt the hard catch of pavement under my tires on the road. I headed up the hill to pick up my last mail at the Lake Parker General Store. There was no mail for me, but as I walked out onto the dusty slats of the porch, nothing more to do before turning the car south, I felt as though I'd just received a very long letter, one I'd written to myself, one it would take me years and years to read. It told of trees and snow and wind, of silences and open spaces, of the fundamental compromise and glory of being a human being, and of other things I hadn't understood at the time, and perhaps would only be able to understand later, in the years to come.

I drove through Barton once more, just to pass the C&C, and the café, still closed, and then I followed the road back to the highway, turned onto the ramp heading south, and allowed myself, not without a mixture of relief and regret, to pick up speed.

Acknowledgments

Gratitude is the happiest form of debt—the accounts are in-calculable, and the only way to square them is by trying to do good work and by trying to be generous in the ways others have been generous to you. In other words, I will forever be working to repay:

My family: Mom, Dad, and Matt, all of whom supported this book without knowing what was in it, which means, really, that they supported me. The years the book contains, and the years it took to write, weren't easy on any of us, and their love helped me more than I can say.

My early mentors: Robert Coles and Ron Carlson—for their examples, their profound decency, and their encourage-ment. Thanks also to Alison Hawthorne Deming, Jane Miller, Steve Orlen, Boyer Rickel, and everyone at the University of Arizona MFA program.

The residencies where I wrote so much of the book: Ucross, Blue Mountain Center, Virginia Center for the Creative Arts, Kimmel Harding Nelson, the Anderson Center, the Norman Mailer Center, Hambidge, and the Vermont Studio Center. Special thanks to Harriet Barlow, Ben Strader, Ruth Salvatore, Sharon Dynak, and Gary Clark.

My early readers, for their insights and their belief in the project: Susan Choi, David Ebershoff, Albert LaFarge, Caryn Cardello, Julie Bloemeke, Cornelius Howland, Jill Gallenstein, Aaron Goldberg, Leah Gillis, Peter Derby, Chris Boucher, Katherine Cohen, and Aaron Richmond.

My later readers: Tanya Larkin, Helena de Bres, and Mary Marbourg, for their keen intellectual responses to the ideas and their deeply felt personal responses to the emotions.

The community: everyone at Grub Street, especially Chip Cheek, Chris Castellani, Sonya Larson, Alison Murphy, Sean Van Deuren, Lauren Rheaume, and to James Scott for bringing me into the fold. To my memoir students, who, through their own writing, reminded me of what memoir can do. And to my students at the University of Arizona, Wentworth Institute of Technology, and Framingham State, whose questions about the book helped me understand the story I was telling. And to my WIT colleagues: Devon Sprague, Max Grinnell, and Loren Sparling.

For behind-the-scenes understanding and guidance: Linda Madoff, Jami Axelrod, Alicia Pritt, Jodi Heyman, Shuchi Saraswat, Jaime Clark, Mary Cotton, Bill McKibben, Wendy Wakeman, Vicki Kennedy, Doris Cooper, Katherine Fausset, Leslie Jamison, Adelle Waldman, David Macmillan, and Bill Hayes. And to Sophie Barbasch, for the photograph and for all the great cartoons.

A special thank-you to Anne LeClaire, for reading an early draft and believing in it enough to introduce me to her agent, Deborah Schneider, and to Bella Pollen, for being such a kind and generous reader.

And to Oliver Sacks, for his insight, his kindness, and for giving the book the highest compliment it could possibly receive.

To Charles Bock, for guiding me through every stage, including that talk in Central Park before my meetings with agents and for being such a smart and abiding friend. A mensch in every possible way.

To Deborah Schneider, my superhero agent, who saw the book I was writing even when I couldn't and who always knew how and when to fight. She was the fearless advocate this project needed, and she earned my trust in hundreds of ways. Thanks also to Victoria Marini and to everyone at Gelfman Schneider/ ICM Partners and Curtis Brown in London.

To Alexis Rizzuto, my editor, for her immediate and intuitive understanding of the book and for her tireless attention to detail. Also, to Helene Atwan, Tom Hallock, Rob Arnold, Will Myers, and the whole team at Beacon Press. I'm so proud to be on the Beacon list.

To Ray Hearey, who I thought of so often while writing and whose friendship was always with me, even from across the country.

To Andrew Rueb, a true friend through everything. For all the dinners, all the talks, all the faith. And for all the understanding, without needing to read a word.

And, lastly, one more thank-you to my parents. This book, in so many ways, is for you.